CONTENTS

KU-163-970

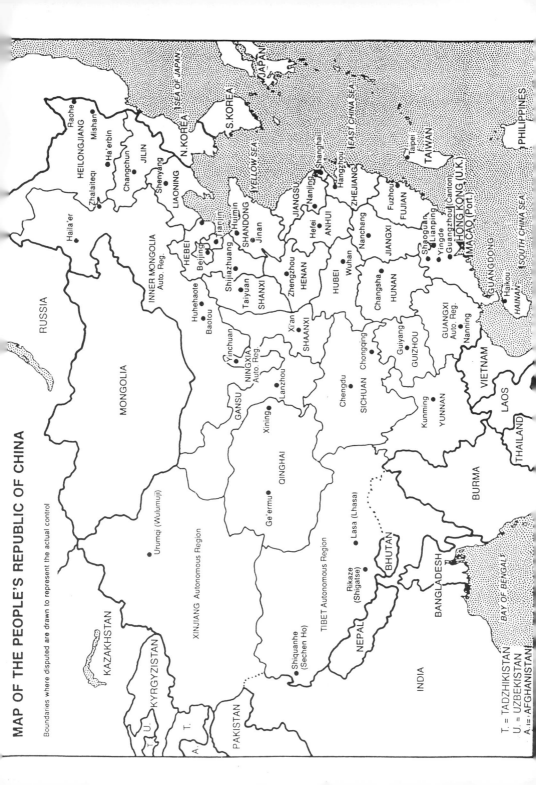

MAP OF THE PEOPLE'S REPUBLIC OF CHINA

Boundaries where disputed are drawn to represent the actual control

T. = TADZHIKISTAN
U. = UZBEKISTAN
A. = AFGHANISTAN

INTRODUCTION

NO ONE IS SAFE

Liang Rihua was arrested in May 1993 on suspicion of stealing chickens. A few hours later he had been tortured to death by police determined he should confess. Phuntsog Yangkyi, a 20-year-old Tibetan nun, was jailed for five years in 1992 for joining a peaceful demonstration in support of Tibetan independence. In 1994 she was reportedly beaten severely by guards after she and other nuns sang nationalist songs. She died in a police hospital a few months later.

These stories, like the many others detailed in this report, show that no one is safe in China. They are also a reminder of the personal dimension to human rights violations in China, often obscured by its vast size and long history of political repression. The fundamental rights of people like Liang Rihua and Phuntsog Yangkyi are no less important because they happen to be one in a billion.

Despite the dramatic changes that have taken place in China in the past decade, human rights violations continue on a massive scale. Many of the abuses result from official policies and repressive legislation that curtail fundamental rights and freedoms. Others are committed in breach of Chinese law itself as officials exercise their power arbitrarily and, often, with impunity.

Dissent and any activity perceived as a threat to the established political order continue to be repressed. Thousands of political opponents and members of religious and ethnic groups are in jail, many simply for expressing their beliefs. Often they face grossly unfair trials, with guilty verdicts decided long before they reach court. Countless people are held in administrative detention for years without ever being charged. Despite increased official tolerance of debate about legal reforms, human rights defenders are ruthlessly persecuted.

Torture is common in detention centres and prisons, causing many deaths each year. It is used to extract confessions, or to punish, coerce or intimidate political and criminal prisoners. Although Chinese law prohibits some forms of torture, the authorities have failed to introduce the most basic safeguards to prevent torture, or to bring many torturers to justice. This suggests that torture often results from institutionalized practices and official policies. Social programs such as the birth control policy are administered in ways that involve coercion and ill-treatment. Some women are abducted by local officials and forced to have abortions or undergo sterilization.

The death penalty is widely used to instil fear into the population, particularly during crackdowns on crime. Thousands of people are sentenced to death each year. Many of them are executed, often without any legal safeguards against miscarriages of justice. Increasing numbers are being put to death for non-violent offences.

The context in which these human rights violations take place is unique. The Chinese Government rules a diverse population of

Traditional methods of agriculture continue in Menghan, Yunnan province, while (right) skyscrapers dominate the city of Shenzhen.
© Michael Yamashita/Colorific!

more than 1.2 billion, including over 50 officially recognized ethnic groups speaking dozens of languages. In some regions the economy is highly developed while others have hardly been touched by modern technology. There are huge areas in which the people have almost no contact with the outside world and about which virtually nothing is known. This century, the country has survived the traumas of foreign invasion, civil war and revolution.

China's great population and limited resources present its authorities with the difficult challenge of generating the sustainable development needed to deliver basic economic rights to all the people. The past 15 years have seen some remarkable achievements in this respect. With an annual growth rate of about 10 per cent, China has become one of the world's largest economies, a leading international trader and a powerful magnet for investment.

The economic changes have significantly improved the level of social and economic freedom for many people. A growing entrepreneurial class is enjoying greater riches and freedoms. In many areas, work units no longer exert the same control over everyday life. Lines of communication both internally and externally have expanded and diversified. New opportunities exist for foreign education and travel.

But the economic reforms have also given rise to problems. Inflation is rampant. Disparities have opened up between coastal and inland provinces, and between urban and rural areas. The gap between rich and poor has also widened, creating new social tensions. An estimated 70 million people — more than the population of many countries — make up a "floating" population of rural migrants seeking work in the cities. Often poor and ill-educated, they are frequently blamed by the authorities for China's social problems, particularly rising levels of crime. Corruption has become rife.

Despite the economic changes, the formal political structures governing China remain virtually unaltered. Almost all senior government and administrative posts are held by members or leaders of the Chinese Communist Party (CCP) and all major policy decisions are taken by the Party. The National People's Congress (NPC), the country's legislature, still has little power. The judiciary

A crowded street in Guangzhou: China's 1.2 billion population presents the authorities with the difficult challenge of meeting the economic needs of all the people. © Rex Features

Prisoners convicted of economic crimes being paraded in a truck through the streets of Guangzhou. © *SIPA/Rex Features*

remains under the influence of the CCP and political interference is in-built into aspects of the judicial process. Devolution of some regulatory powers has given provincial governments more control over certain local issues. Administrations in the more prosperous provinces enjoy greater autonomy in managing their economies. Provincial administrations have been interpreting laws according to local needs.

Overall, economic development has led to few improvements in China's human rights record. Despite some new laws aimed at redressing human rights violations, political repression and the arbitrary exercise of power remain systemic. There is no sign of fundamental changes in the official human rights policy or in aspects of the legal system which foster gross and systematic human rights violations.

The Chinese authorities have sought to avoid criticism and scrutiny of China's human rights record by the UN and international human rights organizations. In international human rights debates, they have repeatedly asserted that human rights issues are a matter of national sovereignty; arguing that no one has the right to interfere in another country's internal affairs. They reject the vital principle, established by international law and the practice of all states working collectively in the UN, that the promotion and protection of human rights are matters of international concern.

The principle of state sovereignty is not incompatible with the principle of international cooperation on human rights. Furthermore, sovereignty should not mean giving power to law enforcers and other officials to disregard with impunity both domestic laws and international human rights standards. The government is accountable, under both domestic and international law, to stop the serious human rights violations being committed as a result of abuse of power, arbitrary implementation of the law and repressive legislation.

As China plays an increasingly prominent role in world affairs, including in trade and in UN and regional intergovernmental structures, it must accept the responsibilities that come with it. In today's globalized world, China cannot make human rights an exception or violate them with impunity.

This report documents the patterns of violations in China in recent years. It describes the individual tragedies of people who have been jailed for exercising their fundamental rights, as well as

Attempts by Chinese people to speak out for reforms have been met with violent repression. Thousands of people join the "Long March for Democracy" in early 1989. © Index on Censorship

many cases of torture, unfair trial and judicial executions. It also analyses why these violations continue to be perpetrated on a massive scale in China.

The report is based on research information gathered over many years and was written in October 1995. The sources include interviews with people who have witnessed or experienced human rights violations in China, official Chinese documents and press reports, and regional and international media reports. Amnesty International takes no position on the politics of the Chinese Government; the organization works to protect and promote human rights in all countries of the world, regardless of the political structures or ideologies. Amnesty International's sole aim is to end violations of the specific political and civil rights which fall within its mandate for action. To this end, Amnesty International urges the Chinese authorities to take immediate and effective action to protect the lives, dignity and safety of all China's citizens.

The world cannot ignore the human rights of a fifth of its people. What happens in China is an important measure of the state of human rights internationally. The international community must insist that the Chinese Government fulfils its human rights obligations. For China's business and development partners, improvements in human rights are crucial to the long-term political and economic stability of the country. For China's 1.2 billion people, such improvements can mean the difference between life and death.

1

The law and abuse of power

Arbitrariness prevails in the enforcement of law in China. Every year, countless numbers of people are detained without charge in breach of the law or sentenced without trial to years of "re-education through labour" at the discretion of police or local officials. For those who are charged, sentences are frequently imposed after unfair trials, with the verdict decided beforehand, and in many cases such verdicts carry the death penalty.

The Chinese legal system, like all legal systems, supports the established political and governmental institutions. But it does not do so in a way that is consistent with the rule of law and fundamental human rights. The rule of law is subordinate to higher political goals, including the defeat of perceived political enemies. The vagueness and contradictory provisions of the law lead consistently to its arbitrary use and provide wide scope for the abuse of power. Repressive criminal legislation and the extensive system of administrative detention mean that anyone can be detained at the whim of individuals in a position of power. The judiciary lacks independence and the judicial process is subject to interference by political authorities.

The case of Yan Zhengxue illustrates the arbitrariness and double standards with which the law can be applied in China. On 2 July 1993 Yan Zhengxue was tortured by three policemen at the Haidian district police station in Beijing, suffering injuries which were recorded in a hospital report immediately after the assault (see Chapter 4). Two weeks later, he filed a suit against his attackers with the Haidian district People's Court. The court apparently carried out a preliminary investigation and questioned the three policemen. According to Yan Zhengxue's lawyer, a written record of this interrogation shows that all three admitted involvement in the assault to different degrees. Soon after the Haidian Public Security Sub-bureau reportedly offered to arrange compensation for Yan Zhengxue if he dropped the case. He refused. Months passed without the court taking any action to hear the case.

After Yan Zhengxue's attempts to bring his torturers to justice had gained widespread public support, the court eventually heard the case in early April 1994, although only one of Yan Zhengxue's assailants was prosecuted. Yan Zhengxue was reportedly not allowed to testify and the doctor who had examined him at the Xiyuan hospital was not called. The police officer on trial, Zhang Chi, was sentenced to a one-year suspended prison sentence and asked to pay unspecified compensation.

Yan Zhengxue, however, suffered immediate retribution for the policeman's trial: he was detained a few days afterwards on a trumped-up accusation. In September 1993 colleagues of the police officers he was suing had accused him of "stealing" a bicycle. There was no evidence of the alleged theft and Yan Zhengxue was never

A plainclothes police officer attacks and beats a man during arrest while a uniformed officer looks on, Guangzhou, August 1994. © Rex Features

charged. Despite this, on 21 April 1994 a committee of the Beijing municipal government used the accusation to sentence him, without formal charge or trial, to two years of "re-education through labour".

The double standards applied in this case are clear. In contrast to the police officer convicted of torturing him, who was tried before a court of law and granted the right to defence, Yan Zhengxue was sentenced by a local government committee and was prevented from refuting the accusation against him. While the policeman received a suspended sentence and walked free, Yan Zhengxue was sent to a forced labour camp. Ultimately, he was arbitrarily punished for trying to exercise his right to seek justice against officials who abused their power, a right guaranteed by the Chinese Constitution and law.

Unease at such cases of injustice and arbitrary punishments has provoked debates in Chinese academic and legal circles about the "rule of law" versus "rule by people". In recent years, some scholars have advocated far-reaching legal reforms. In 1994, for example, detailed "viewpoints" for reform of the Criminal Law were made by academics at a national symposium and published in the national newspaper, the *Legal Daily*. They included recommendations on reducing the scope of the death penalty and giving more severe punishments to state functionaries who committed "crimes of dereliction of duty" — in other words, who abused their power.

The authorities have made some responses to calls for legal reform. The State Compensation Law, adopted in May 1994, gives citizens the right to seek compensation against infringements of their "legitimate rights and interests" by state organizations or functionaries. The Prison Law, adopted in December 1994, reiterates the prohibition of torture and ill-treatment of prisoners already included in the Criminal Law. Some provisional regulations concerning complaints against the police, promulgated by the Public Security Ministry in January 1995, grant citizens the right to present suits or appeals directly to public security bodies for violation of the law or "dereliction of duty" by police officials and public security bodies.

However, these reforms do not fundamentally change the system which provides for arbitrary detention and imprisonment. A vast array of laws and regulations continues to be used to detain or imprison political opponents or to warn potential dissidents against opposition. The laws also contain procedural

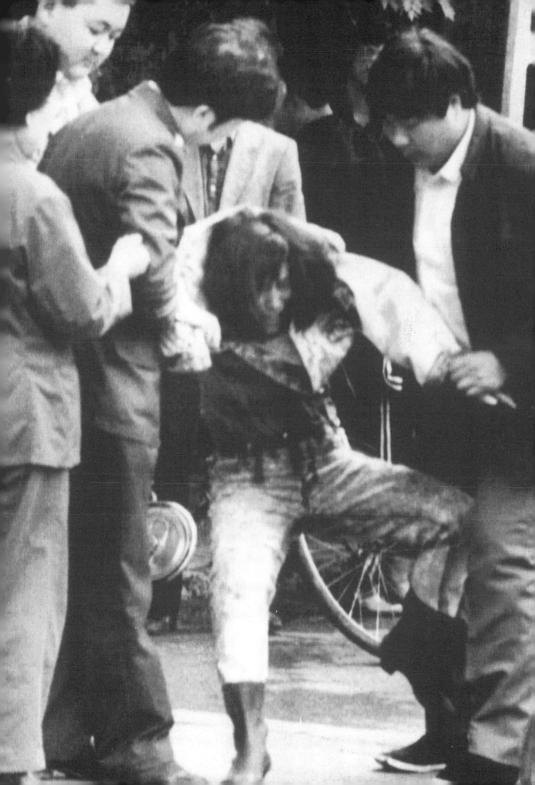

provisions which foster other human rights violations. Moreover, new laws have been adopted which curtail fundamental freedoms even further.

The law as a tool of political repression

The Chinese authorities say there are no political prisoners in China. This is not true. People are routinely imprisoned because of their political views or beliefs, but are categorized as "counter-revolutionaries", administrative detainees or common criminals. In January 1995, for instance, a Ministry of Justice official was cited as stating that 2,678 prisoners convicted of "counter-revolutionary" offences were currently in jail. Amnesty International believes that this figure represents only a fraction of the real number of political prisoners. It excludes many thousands of people who are jailed for political reasons but convicted of other offences, or held under various forms of administrative detention without charge or trial, or detained for long periods for investigation pending trial.

Criminal Law

China had virtually no criminal legislation until 1979, when the Criminal Law and Criminal Procedure Law (CPL) were adopted. Drafted during a period of "liberalization" after the massive abuses of the Cultural Revolution, the new laws introduced in principle some protection for individual rights. However, they also contain provisions which make human rights violations an inherent aspect of the legal system.

The Criminal Law contains a section on "crimes of counter-revolution", defined as all acts "committed with the goal of over-throwing the political power of the dictatorship of the proletariat and the socialist system". It provides for punishments ranging from "deprivation of political rights" (which means the person cannot vote or stand for official office, and frequently includes restrictions on movement) to the death penalty for 12 "counter-revolutionary"

Page 12: *An inmate of Haicheng rehabilitation camp, following an attempted escape.* © *Xinhua/Frank Spooner*

Page 13: *A year after the pro-democracy demonstrations in June 1989, police officers arrest a woman near Tiananmen Square in Beijing. A vast array of laws and regulations is used by the Chinese authorities to detain or imprison political opponents and to deter potential dissidents.* © *Reuters* offences. The provisions which are most often used to jail prisoners of conscience — people held because of their beliefs, or because of their ethnic origin, sex, colour, language, national or social origin, economic status, birth or other status, who have not used or advocated violence — are contained in Articles 98 and 102. The first provides punishments for "organizing, leading or taking part in a counter-revolutionary group", which effectively applies to any group which is critical of government policy or is simply not officially recognized. The second prohibits "counter-revolutionary propaganda and incitement", which effectively bans the expression of dissenting social, political or religious views. Two other articles which deal with "plots to subvert the government" and "the use of feudal superstition or superstitious sects and secret societies to carry out counter-revolutionary activities" are also frequently used to jail prisoners of conscience.

Prisoners of conscience have also been jailed under other

A notice posted in Shanghai warning that demonstrations are damaging to the city's well-being. Provisions in criminal law permit prosecution and conviction of anyone whose words or actions can be construed as disruptive of public order. © SIPA/Rex Features

provisions in the Criminal Law. For example, they have been imprisoned on charges of "disturbing public order", "hooliganism", "harbouring counter-revolutionary elements or giving false proof to protect them", or "assembling a crowd to disturb public order". The vague language of many of these provisions permits the prosecution and conviction of anyone whose words, actions or associations can be construed as disruptive of public order or critical of official policies.

Since the late 1980s some Chinese legal scholars have advocated repeal of the provisions on "counter-revolutionary crimes" and proposed that these be replaced by measures that focus on national security. These proposals are said to be under consideration, but little is known about any proposed changes or the progress of discussions. While the repeal of these provisions would be welcome, there are reasons to fear that this would not stop arbitrary detention and imprisonment unless further changes were made to legislation and practice.

State Security Law

The State Security Law, adopted in February 1993, and the Detailed Rules for Implementing the State Security Law, adopted in May 1994, both include provisions which restrict fundamental freedoms. The law criminalizes acts "harmful to state security" which are carried out by "organizations, groups or individuals outside the territory", or those "instigated and financed by them" or carried out "in collusion with them" by organizations or individuals inside China (Article 5). The proscribed activities include: "plotting to subvert the government", "espionage", "secretly gathering...and illegally providing state secrets for an enemy", "instigating...state personnel to rise in rebellion" and "other activities against state security".

These "other activities" are defined in Article 8 of the Implementation Rules as acts which involve the exercise of fundamental freedoms — such as freedom of speech, publication, association and religion — when these "endanger state security". The Rules do not specify the circumstances in which such activities would constitute a "danger to state security", but, in the light of Article 1 of the law, this means any activity perceived as a threat to the established political order. The Rules make it a criminal offence for people in China to have contacts with or receive financial support from any organization, within or outside the country, defined as "hostile to the People's Republic of China (PRC) government and socialist system characterized by the people's dictatorship, as well as those which endanger state security". In other words, the law is designed primarily to protect the political authorities and their policies, rather than the security of the state.

These provisions are applicable to a broad range of potential and actual political opponents, as well as to anyone deemed to be a threat because of their contacts with unapproved individuals or organizations, or because they are dealing with issues the government considers a threat, including human rights. This legislation has so far mainly been invoked against people accused of leaking "state secrets".

State secrets law

Since 1991 a growing number of people whom Amnesty International considers to be prisoners of conscience, including journalists, have been arrested and sentenced on charges of "leaking state secrets".

Soldiers stand guard as a Tibetan woman walks around the Barkor circuit at the Jokhang temple in Lhasa. Many fundamental freedoms, such as freedom of religion, are severely curtailed in China.
© Springer-Liaison/Frank Spooner

REFERENCE & INFORMATION LIBRARY HUMANITIES WORCESTERSHIRE COUNTY LIBRARIES AND INFORMATION SERVICE

Bao Tong was sentenced in 1992 to seven years in prison for "leaking state secrets". His case illustrates how legislation on state secrets can be used for political ends.

The case of Bao Tong illustrates how the legislation on state secrets is used arbitrarily for political ends. Bao Tong was a close assistant of the former CCP Secretary General, Zhao Ziyang, who resigned shortly before the imposition of martial law in Beijing on 20 May 1989. Bao Tong was arrested soon after, on 28 May 1989. He was then a member of the CCP Central Committee (CCPCC) and Director of the CCPCC Research Centre for Reform of the Political Structure. Within the centre, he had reportedly initiated a draft scheme for political reform, which was opposed by anti-reform elements in the CCP leadership. The sentence passed on Bao Tong, more than three years after his arrest, appears to have been an act of political retribution rather than proper implementation of the state secrets law. Indeed, the decision to sentence him is reported to have been taken directly by the CCP leadership.

Following his arrest, Bao Tong was accused of "revealing Party secrets". He was held for a year in solitary confinement at Qincheng prison, then released into house arrest in May 1990. On 21 January 1992 he was rearrested and sentenced on 21 July 1992 to a seven-year prison term after a closed trial.

According to the court verdict, the charge that he "leaked state secrets" is based solely on a private conversation he had with another senior CCP official on the evening of 17 May 1989. The verdict gives no indication of the nature of the "important state secret situation" which Bao Tong allegedly leaked to this colleague, but information from other sources indicates this is related to the impending declaration of martial law and the resignation of Zhao Ziyang as CCP Secretary General, both of which were made public on 20 May 1989. Another charge against Bao Tong, "counter-revolutionary propaganda and incitement", is based on the accusation that he "indicated assent" to having the transcript of part of a private conversation with a senior official on 20 May 1989 made available to others. Amnesty International considers Bao Tong to be a prisoner of conscience.

The 1988 Law on the Protection of State Secrets defines state secrets as being "matters that affect the security and interests of the state". These include conventional matters of national security, such as national defence and diplomatic affairs. However, they also include "secrets concerning important policy decisions on

Bai Weiji and his wife Zhao Lei were sentenced after an unfair trial to terms in prison for "leaking state secrets".

19

state affairs", "national economy and social development secrets" and "other state secrets". This definition is made even broader by another provision, according to which "secrets of political parties" are also considered "state secrets" if they are deemed to "affect the security and interests of the state". This effectively bans public reporting or debate of any issue concerning the CCP whenever the Party's authorities decide they should not be disclosed.

The 1990 Procedures for Implementing the Law of the PRC on the Protection of State Secrets further stipulate that if the disclosure of information on certain matters results in a number of "consequences", this information should be classified as a state secret. Eight consequences are defined, including "endangering the consolidation and defence of the state political power", and "affecting state unification, national unity and social stability". This refers potentially to any information that is deemed liable to undermine the authority of the government or to trigger social discontent or ethnic unrest. In 1993 the maximum punishment for those who "steal, secretly gather, buy or illegally provide state secrets for organizations, groups or individuals outside the territory" was raised to the death penalty; previously it had been seven years' imprisonment.

The legislation on state secrets, like the state security laws, is largely designed to protect the interests of the political authorities, rather than genuine state secrets. It has been increasingly used to arbitrarily repress freedom of expression and association.

Administrative detention: a major source of abuse

"Those who wield executive power tend to regard laws as decorative — and not as legally binding as the administrative regulations."
Zhang Weiguo, 4 June 1993[1]

Guarantees against arbitrary arrest and detention set down in laws passed by the legislature in China are undermined and contradicted by executive decrees and regulations providing for administrative detention. Amnesty International has described these in detail in the past.[2]

The two major forms of administrative detention which cause widespread human rights violations in China are "shelter and investigation" (*shourong jiancha*) and "re-education through labour" (*laodong jiaojang*). Both clearly breach international human rights standards, notably the principle that no one may be kept in detention without being given an effective opportunity to have his or her case heard promptly by a judicial or similar authority.[3] They also violate rights guaranteed by other international standards, including the right to be held according to the law and the right of access to lawyers and families. The vagueness and confusion surrounding some of the Chinese regulations covering administrative detention add to the risks of arbitrary application. With such a catalogue of failings, it is clear that many people in China are being arbitrarily detained under these forms of administrative detention in violation of international law, including many political prisoners.

"Shelter and investigation" is a form of preventive detention. It allows the police, on their own authority, to detain people without charge for up to three months, merely on the suspicion that they may be involved in crime. It bypasses the procedures for arrest and detention provided for in the CPL and is imposed by the police without any judicial supervision or review. In theory, it applies to people suspected of "minor acts of law-infringement or crime" whose "general background" or "true names and addresses" are unclear. In practice, it is frequently used to detain people who do not fit this definition and many are held for longer than the permitted three months, some of them for several years. For instance, Zhang Weiguo, a prominent journalist from Shanghai, was illegally detained under these provisions for six months in 1989 before being formally arrested. He said that at the Shanghai detention centre where he was held, there were other detainees who had been held arbitrarily for more than three years.

Various sources indicate that several hundred thousand people have been detained every year for "shelter and investigation" since the 1980s. In 1991 the Ministry of Public Security reportedly stated that there were 930,000 such cases in 1989 and 902,000 in 1990.[4] According to Chinese legal scholars, official statistics show that only a small proportion of those held — 10 per cent in some areas — have actually broken the law,[5] and some 30 to 40 per cent are held beyond the permitted limit of three months.

The majority of those held for "shelter and investigation" are the less educated or less privileged, particularly rural migrants and workers. Often they are detained by corrupt police officers who ask for heavy fines as a condition for release. "Shelter and investigation" is also used to detain political dissidents or to coerce people

involved in economic disputes — usually when there is no evidence to justify arresting them under the Criminal Law.

Some detainees held for "shelter and investigation" are subsequently assigned a term of "re-education through labour", a punishment imposed by local government committees for up to three years, renewable by one year.[6] It is applied to people considered to have "anti-socialist views" or those whose "crimes" are "too minor" to be prosecuted under the Criminal Law. They are not charged with a crime or tried, and have no access to a lawyer and no chance of defending themselves.

"Re-education through labour" was introduced under a Decision adopted by the government in 1957. The Decision was updated in 1979 and subsequent years, but no attempt was made to bring it into line with the criminal legislation introduced in 1979. According to Article 48 of the CPL, no one may be detained without charge for more than 10 days. Yet, according to official figures, well over 100,000 people are held in labour "re-education" camps at any one time. Since 1989, these have included hundreds of dissidents and members of religious or ethnic groups. Together with "shelter and investigation", the "re-education through labour" system provides a convenient way for the authorities to arbitrarily jail dissidents and others without having to justify their detention through the judicial process.

Some Chinese legal scholars and judicial officials have challenged the legality of these two forms of detention, arguing that they conflict with China's criminal legislation which should prevail over executive decrees. They have also pointed out that there is a chaotic maze of contradictory official documents and regulations concerning both forms of detention, and questioned the legal status of some of them as they are not published. Legal scholars have also criticized the two forms of detention as being the source of many abuses, including torture.

In 1990 a new law was introduced allowing an appeal before the courts. However, it involves a long and cumbersome process that is in practice inaccessible to many detainees. The new law does

---

Page 22: *A labour camp in the Hangkou district of Wuhan City, Hubei province, where shoes are made by the prisoners.* © *Dr Thomas Weyrauch*

Page 23: *A labour camp in northern China. In many labour camps, prisoners are subjected to hard physical labour and ill-treated if they do not fulfil work quotas or "repent" their crimes.* © *SRKC/Katz Pictures*

not prevent arbitrary detention without charge or trial and does not fundamentally change the system of widespread administrative detention. Furthermore, in political cases, the courts' decisions seem to be guided by political considerations: no dissident held under an administrative detention order has yet won an appeal, even when the grounds for detention were shown to be false.[7]

Arbitrariness in the criminal process

Wei Jingsheng © Adrian Bradshaw

Wei Jingsheng, an outspoken critic of the government and former prisoner of conscience, was arrested in Beijing in April 1994 during a wave of arrests of dissidents in the capital. He was believed to have been detained for expressing his views on human rights and political issues and for having contacts with foreigners, including the US Assistant Secretary of State for Human Rights. His treatment highlights the vast scope for arbitrary detention that is allowed by the CPL.

More than 18 months after his arrest, Wei Jingsheng was still being held at an undisclosed location outside Beijing. The authorities had not made public any charges against him. Nor had they informed his family of the reasons for his detention or allowed them to visit him. Official sources reportedly stated that Wei Jingsheng had been placed under "supervised residence" (*jianshi juzhu*, literally "living at home under surveillance"). However, Wei Jingsheng was manifestly not living at home.

"Supervised residence" is arbitrarily used by the authorities to restrict people either at home or in a designated area or place, such as a government "guest house". For the prisoner the result is total isolation. For the authorities, it provides total control of all information about the prisoner, which is not always possible in legitimate places of detention.

There is no legal time limit for "supervised residence". According to Article 44 of the CPL, "supervised residence" can be applied to "a person whom it is necessary to arrest [charge] but against whom there is not yet sufficient evidence". In the case of people like Wei Jingsheng, this may mean arbitrary, indefinite and incommunicado detention without charge.

The provisions of the CPL, which limit detention without charge to 10 days, are seldom respected. Hundreds of political detainees have been arbitrarily detained for weeks or months before charges were brought. The CPL also contains various loopholes and vague provisions that are effectively used to nullify the few protections for individual rights included in the law. For example, Article 43 stipulates that "the family of the detained person or his unit should be notified within 24 hours after detention of the reasons for detention and the place of custody", but this can be ignored if "notification would hinder the investigation or there is no way to notify them". In hundreds of cases of political prisoners known to Amnesty International, the families were not notified for months of the reasons for or place of detention.

A further loophole concerns the legally prescribed period of investigation — that is, the period of time between formal arrest (charge) and the initiation of public prosecution. This should normally take no more than five and a half months, depending on the complexity of the case (Articles 92, 97 and 99). However, a clause in Article 92 makes it possible in "especially major and complex cases" to postpone prosecution for an unspecified period, with the approval of the Standing Committee of the NPC or local people's congresses. Since 1989, many political prisoners have been held for investigation for far longer than five and a half months before being brought to trial, some for over two years.

The potential for abuse is increased by the fact that the law does not grant detainees the right of access to lawyers or to a judicial authority until a few days before their trial. They therefore have no means of challenging the legality of their detention and may, in effect, "disappear" in the system.

Unfair trials

In November 1994 Gao Yu, a well-known journalist in China, was convicted of "leaking important state secrets" in articles she had written for two Hong Kong magazines. She was sentenced after a secret trial to six years in prison and a further year's deprivation of political rights. Her husband and lawyers were not informed of the trial. The verdict indicated that the "state secrets" in question concerned political and not national security issues. Moreover, all the evidence suggests that the court had condemned Gao Yu before her trial.

Prior to the announcement of the verdict, Gao Yu was brought to trial three times in 1994. Each time the court found that the evidence against her "still needed to be verified" — meaning that the prosecution evidence was

Gao Yu, a well-known journalist, was imprisoned for six years in November 1994 after a series of grossly unfair judicial proceedings.
© China Rights Forum

insufficient to convict her. On three occasions the court returned her case to the Beijing procuracy "for supplementary investigation and verification". Throughout these proceedings, the court ignored the information and arguments presented by the defence, which challenged the validity of the evidence against Gao Yu.[8] Amnesty International believes that Gao Yu is a prisoner of conscience jailed solely for the peaceful exercise of her right to freedom of expression.

Gao Yu's story is not unusual. In political cases the verdict is decided before trial. This practice, widely known in China as "verdict first, trial second", can apply in ordinary criminal cases as well. It violates the fundamental principles of international law and has been publicly criticized by members of the Chinese legal profession since the mid-1980s.[9] Despite this, the practice continues.

The right to be presumed innocent before being proved guilty is a fundamental principle of international law. Countries are free

A man standing trial before a court accused of stealing a television set. Many trials in China are grossly unfair, particularly in political cases where the verdict is often decided before trial. © *Hu Yong/Frank Spooner*

to develop their own trial procedures, provided they fulfil minimum standards for fair trial set out in international law. International standards require a trial without too much delay that is open to the public except in very limited circumstances, adequate time and facilities for the accused to prepare a defence and to consult a lawyer of the defendant's choice, and the right during trial to cross-examine witnesses and hear evidence from defence witnesses.

In China, the determination of guilt and sentence is usually decided outside the trial court by committees subject to political interference. Under the CPL "all major and difficult cases" are submitted for discussion and decision to the court's "adjudication committee" (*shenpan weiyuanhui*) when the court president deems it "necessary" (Article 107). These committees are set up in each court to supervise judicial work and, according to Chinese judges, consist of the court president (usually a CCP member) and other members of the CCP committee of the court.[10]

The adjudication committees make decisions on the basis of files and without the presence of the defendant or defence lawyers. Other authorities, including the CCP political and law committees, may also issue opinions to the courts. Whereas only important criminal cases are handled in this way, such interference is systematic in political cases.

Even if there is no interference, trials are often a mere formality. In the overwhelming majority of cases known to Amnesty International, court verdicts are almost verbatim reproductions of the indictments presented by prosecutors and take virtually no account of the defence. In all cases, the right to defence is severely limited. Defence witnesses are rarely allowed to give evidence in court, although they can in theory be called. There is no presumption of innocence and the burden of proof is on the defence. Defendants who are brought to trial have usually spent months detained incommunicado, subjected to pressure by the investigating authorities and without access to a lawyer. Detainees can seek the assistance of a lawyer only after a court has decided to try the case — usually months after arrest and just a few days before trial. The right of lawyers to meet detainees and the power to challenge the findings of the prosecution are also limited.

In practice, lawyers have access to only a part of the file concerning a defendant. They usually cannot confront prosecution witnesses and are effectively barred from challenging the validity of the charges. In many cases, therefore, they merely call for mitigation of the sentence. This is particularly so with lawyers appointed by the courts, which happens when the defendants have no means of appointing their own counsel. Furthermore, not all defendants have a lawyer. They may not know of their right to have one or may simply believe it is futile.

An obedient judiciary

An independent and impartial judiciary is the cornerstone of the right to a fair trial in international law. Judicial independence does not exist in China. The 1982 Constitution states that the courts shall be free from interference by "administrative organizations, public bodies and individuals". This definition does not prohibit interference by political authorities. It was integrated in 1983 into the Organic Law of the People's Courts, replacing a clause stating that the courts are "subordinate only to the law".

During the late 1980s, a more open political climate led to debates about the legal system and criticisms of the CCP's interference in the courts' work. Calls for reforms were made by some members of the legal profession and there were signs of increased judicial independence. This trend was reversed after the 1989 crackdown on pro-democracy protests. On 20 June 1989 the Supreme People's Court issued a circular instructing local courts "to act and think in line with Comrade Deng Xiaoping", and to "try promptly" and mete out "severe punishment" to those who had "created the social turmoil".

Since then, other statements have reaffirmed the leading role of the political authorities in judicial work. In March 1995, for example, the report of Procurator General Zhang Siqing to the NPC stated: "We should closely rely on the leadership of the Party committees and voluntarily accept supervision by the people's congresses. Procuratorial bodies should regularly report to Party committees and the people's congresses, seek their advice and conscientiously carry out their instructions and opinions."[11] The same month the Supreme People's Court President, Ren Jianxin, also referred to the courts as being "led by the Party".[12]

2

Imprisoning those who speak out

Tang Yuanjuan, an assistant engineer at a car factory, is serving 20 years in prison in Liaon-. ing province for organizing a small discussion group with some friends and a protest march in Changchun city, Jilin province, following the 1989 crackdown. He is just one of nearly 3,000 people Amnesty International has been able to identify since 1989 who have been jailed for political reasons. The total number of people detained on such grounds is believed to be much higher. Only a small proportion of those arrested can be identified and, because of the severe control imposed by the authorities over information concerning human rights issues, only a tiny fraction of arbitrary arrests are reported. Many of the victims are prisoners of conscience.

Anyone who speaks out for their rights in China is likely to suffer violations of their human rights. Some are punished under sweeping legislation that virtually outlaws any expression of dissent. Others are victims of officials who abuse the law and their authority to silence or intimidate those who try to defend their rights. Time and again the authorities have demonstrated that they are willing to use any means, whether legal or illegal, to protect the established order, particularly when confronted by rising levels of criticism.

Political dissidents

Thousands of people have been jailed over the past decade for advocating political reforms or forming small political groups. Many were detained following the 1989 crackdown and received long prison sentences for "counter-revolutionary" offences. Among them is Chen Lantao, a marine biologist in Qingdao, who is serving 16 years in prison in Shandong province for criticizing the government's suppression of the Beijing protests in a speech on 8 June 1989. Sun Xiongying, a cadre at a college in Fuzhou city, is serving a term of 18 years in prison in Fujian province for defacing a statue of Mao Zedong and putting up posters protesting against the 4 June 1989 repression. Yu Zhenbin, who worked at the Archives Bureau in Qinghai province, was sentenced to 12 years' imprisonment for making "reactionary speeches" and setting up an opposition group. Zhao Sujian, a cadre at a construction company in Kaifeng, Henan province, received the same term for putting up "reactionary slogans" in the city.

Chinese official sources stated in April 1991 that nearly 800 people had been tried and sentenced in Beijing alone in connection with the 1989 protests. They did not say what happened to the thousands of others who were detained. In fact, many were tried in provincial cities and others were held for long periods without trial.

In the years since 1989 repression has continued, with many dissidents detained annually. In January 1991 Chen Yanbin and

Pro-democracy activists and residents gather in Beijing in early June 1989: many of those arrested during the crackdown on the protests remain in jail.
© *Jonathon Annells*

Zhang Yafei, two young unemployed men, were sentenced in Beijing to 15 and 11 years' imprisonment respectively for carrying out "counter-revolutionary propaganda and incitement" and forming a "counter-revolutionary group". They were accused of writing and distributing a political journal, *Iron Currents*, which "slandered" the rule of the CCP. They were also accused of forming with four other people a political group, the Chinese Revolutionary Democratic Front, which allegedly aimed to "overthrow the leadership of the CCP and the political power of the people's democratic dictatorship".

Since 1989 large-scale arbitrary arrests have been carried out each year around the anniversary of the 4 June massacre. In 1992, for example, many people were arbitrarily arrested in late May and June in Beijing and various provinces. Fifteen of those held in Beijing were jointly indicted in late July 1993 on "counter-revolutionary" charges. This was the largest group of prisoners of conscience to have been indicted together for several years. They included workers, students, lecturers, a medical doctor and a restaurant owner. They were accused of forming four dissident political groups and of writing and printing political leaflets for distribution.

After a series of delays and unfair judicial proceedings, their trial started in July 1994 and the verdict was finally announced in December 1994. Nine of the defendants were sentenced to between three and 20 years in prison, five were found guilty but "exempted from criminal punishment" — they had already spent two and a half years in detention — and one was sentenced to two years of "supervision", which involves restrictions on freedom of movement. Hu Shigen, a 39-year-old former lecturer at the Beijing Languages Institute, received the longest sentence. He was accused of having established in 1991 the Liberal Democratic Party of China (LDPC), of recruiting members and of drafting documents for the LDPC. These included a "Statement on the Question of Human Rights in China". He was also accused of involvement in other underground groups and of planning to distribute "counter-revolutionary" leaflets prior to 4 June 1992. Detained in Beijing on 28 May 1992, he was illegally held for four months before he was formally arrested and charged. Amnesty International considers him to be a prisoner of conscience.

Other dissidents detained in 1992 were brought to trial in 1993. They included 14 people held in Wuhan, Hubei province, accused of forming in 1991 a political group, the Republican Party, which aimed to establish a multi-party system in China. Zhang Minpeng, the 38-year-old alleged leader of the group, was sentenced in August 1993 to five years' imprisonment on "counter-revolutionary" charges. Arrested in July 1992, he had been illegally held for eight months without charge for "shelter and investigation" before he was formally arrested and charged.

In early 1994 scores of people were arbitrarily detained in Beijing and elsewhere. Unlike many of those held in previous years, they had tried to bring about changes openly within the narrow confines of the law. They had petitioned the authorities, raised cases of injustices and tried openly to form labour rights groups. Arrests of such activists have continued into 1995.

Among those detained was Wei Jingsheng, a former prisoner of conscience who had been released on parole in September 1993 after spending more than 14 years in jail. Arrested in early April 1994, he was still being held without charge more than 18 months later (see Chapter 1). His assistant, Tong Yi, was arrested a few days after him, apparently because she was considered to have been an "accessory". She was sentenced without trial in December 1994 to two and a half years of "re-education through labour" and sent to a labour camp where she was reportedly ill-treated (see Chapter 4).

Human rights defenders

"I am no longer afraid. I have already died once in prison. Once you have been there, you are never really afraid again."

These words were spoken by Ren Wanding a few weeks before he was jailed in June 1989. He is one of many people who have bravely stood up for human rights in China, despite the personal risks. A variety of groups and activities have been organized in recent years attempting to promote and protect human rights; all have been repressed by the government, often using means that flout or abuse Chinese law. Despite the intimidation, new human rights initiatives by individuals and organizations are still being reported on a regular basis.

Ren Wanding, a 49-year-old former accountant, was arrested shortly after the 1989 crackdown and sentenced on 26 January 1991 to seven years' imprisonment on charges of "carrying out counter-revolutionary propaganda and incitement". This was based on

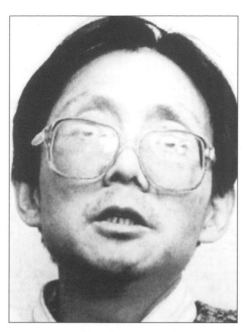

Ren Wanding, a human rights activist arrested in June 1989, and (below) a picture of his earlier arrest in 1979. Since the late 1980s, many people have been jailed for circulating information on human rights issues. Ren Wanding was sentenced to seven years' imprisonment on 26 January 1991 for views he had expressed in speeches and essays during the 1989 pro-democracy movement. © AFP

views he had expressed in speeches and essays during the 1989 pro-democracy movement, in which he called for respect for human rights, free speech and the rule of law. Ren Wanding had been the co-founder of the Chinese Human Rights Alliance, a small group formed in Beijing in late 1978. The group ceased to exist a few months later after its members were arrested. Ren Wanding was detained on 4 April 1979 as he was pasting up a poster on the "democracy wall" and subsequently spent four years in prison. After his release he continued to write and distribute essays on human rights issues.

Since Ren Wanding's most recent arrest, his health has deteriorated considerably. His wife, Zhang Fengying, has appealed to the authorities to improve his conditions of imprisonment and to release him on medical parole. He remains in Beijing Prison No.2.

Since the late 1980s groups of people or individuals have been jailed in Tibet for circulating information about human rights issues. One of them, Gedun Rinchen, was arrested in early May 1993 after writing letters describing the human rights situation in Tibet. He had intended to hand the letters to a delegation of European ambassadors due to arrive in Lhasa, the capital of the Tibet Autonomous Region (TAR), on 16 May. He was accused of "stealing state secrets" and "activities aimed at splitting the country", but was released in January 1994 following international appeals on his behalf. In an earlier case, 10 monks from Drepung monastery and one lay Tibetan received sentences in 1989 ranging from five to 19 years' imprisonment for printing and circulating human rights and political pamphlets. These included a Tibetan translation of the Universal Declaration of Human Rights. One of the monks, 34-year-old Ngawang Phulchung, received the longest sentence as "leader" of the group. Jailed in Drapchi prison in Lhasa, he was among a group of prisoners who were severely beaten by prison guards in April 1991 for protesting at the treatment of other prisoners.

Other jailed human rights defenders include several people who attempted to register a Human Rights Association in Shanghai in 1993. The application was refused by the Shanghai municipal authorities several months later. The group had existed informally since 1978. In May and June 1994 at least eight members of the group were arrested and some were subsequently sentenced to terms of "re-education through labour" without being charged or tried. In March 1994 they had sponsored a petition addressed to the

NPC, written in the name of 54 people from Shanghai, which called for constitutional and human rights reforms. Some members had also reportedly applied to the police authorities for permission to hold a demonstration in May 1994. Li Guotao, a businessman at the Shanghai Computer Development Company and Chairman of the Human Rights Association, was reported to have handed the application to local police shortly before he was arrested.[13]

Another human rights defender who has been jailed in Shanghai since 1994 is Bao Ge, who worked at the Shanghai Medical School. He is said to have been connected to the Shanghai human rights group, but had also campaigned for human rights on his own. He was arrested in June 1994 shortly after sending an open letter to the Chinese Government requesting permission to establish an organization called the Voice of Human Rights. In September 1994 he was sentenced without trial to three years of "re-education through labour" and sent to the Da Feng farm, a labour camp in Jiangsu province where other prisoners of conscience are held. The detention order against Bao Ge stated that he had "disturbed public order".[14]

Bao Ge, a human rights defender, was sentenced without charge or trial to three years' "re-education through labour".

Attempts in other parts of the country to campaign on human rights issues have also been repressed, notably in Xi'an, Shaanxi province.

The intimidation has not silenced the voices demanding respect for human rights. Between March and May 1995, several groups of people in Beijing, including well-known intellectuals and former prisoners of conscience, signed petitions to the authorities calling for more democracy and human rights reforms. One petition, addressed to the NPC in March, urged abolition of the arbitrary system of "shelter and investigation". Another demanded abolition of "re-education through labour", while another called for guarantees for basic human rights. On 15 May a petition signed by 45 people and written by Xu Liangying, a 75-year-old scientist and historian, called for the release of political prisoners and greater tolerance of dissenting views, in reference to a UN decision to make 1995 the UN Year of Tolerance. A few days later another petition called for legal reforms and guarantees of basic human rights, including freedom of the press and association.

More than 50 of these petitioners were detained by police, mainly in Beijing in late May and June 1995. Some of the most prominent signatories were put under pressure by the authorities to withdraw their support for the petitions. Some of those detained were released after interrogation, but at least 10 were reported to be still detained without charge in September 1995. Those released were placed under surveillance and some were instructed to leave Beijing.

The continuing repression of human rights defenders flies in the face of government claims that it is promoting greater debate about human rights. Since 1991 books on human rights have been published in China and formal human rights study groups have been established in several academic institutions. In 1995 the Minister of Justice announced plans to set up a research centre on "justice-related human rights". However, such initiatives, welcome as they are, appear meaningless if ordinary people still face harassment or prison if they try to express human rights concerns.

Workers and labour rights activists

One official trade union exists in China, the All China Federation of Trade Unions (ACFTU). It is the only trade union allowed to represent workers. Those who have attempted to organize independent labour groups or to stand up for workers' rights have been imprisoned or detained without charge. In May 1989, during the pro-democracy movement, groups of workers in various cities formed Workers Autonomous Federations (WAFs) as an alternative to the ACFTU. The WAFs were short-lived: they were banned by the authorities following the 4 June 1989 crackdown and their organizers arrested and prosecuted on "counter-revolutionary" charges. Many other workers who had taken part in the protests were also prosecuted on ordinary criminal charges. Since 1989 there have been other attempts to form independent trade unions or labour rights groups. Again, the organizers have been jailed.

Zhang Jingsheng, a 41-year-old former worker at the Shaoguang Electrical Engineering Plant in Hunan province, is one of many labour activists serving long prison sentences. He was arrested soon after 4 June 1989 and sentenced to 13 years' imprisonment in December 1989 for "counter-revolutionary propaganda

Women workers in a shoe factory in Shanghai. Many labour activists have been imprisoned for exercising their right to free association and speech.
© J Aaronson/Colorific!

LEICESTERSHIRE LIBRARIES AND INFORMATION SERVICE
REFERENCE & INFORMATION LIBRARY
HUMANITIES

Liu Jingsheng (see page 41) *was accused of encouraging workers to form free trade unions. He was sentenced to 15 years' imprisonment in December 1994.*

and incitement". He had spoken at Hunan University about the need for political reform and at a rally in the Martyrs Memorial Park in May 1989 in Changsha, the capital of Hunan province. In late May he became an informal adviser to the newly formed Changsha WAF and allegedly urged workers to go on strike and students to boycott classes. After the crackdown, he reportedly issued an "emergency statement" through the WAF urging resistance to the government's repression. Zhang Jingsheng had been jailed previously as a prisoner of conscience.

In early 1992 another new group, the Preparatory Committee of the Free Labour Union of China (PCFLUC), distributed leaflets in Beijing encouraging workers to form free trade unions. Three or four of the organizers were secretly arrested by plainclothes police officers without warrants in May and June 1992 during large-scale arrests of pro-democracy activists. After the arrests, a letter of appeal from the group reached the International Labour Organisation (ILO) in Geneva. The letter said that workers in China are deprived of their rights of free speech and assembly, and their right to strike. It also spoke of the deterioration of workers' rights since the start of the economic reforms in the late 1970s. It included a commitment to "building an economic and political system of justice and human rights".

One of those arrested was Liu Jingsheng, a worker at the Tongyi Chemical Plant in Tong county, outside Beijing. He was detained on 28 May 1992 and accused of having formed the PCFLUC in December 1991 and of helping to draft materials for the PCFLUC which made a "slanderous accusation" against the CCP. He was also accused of involvement in an underground political group and in writing, printing and planning to distribute pro-democracy leaflets around 4 June 1992. Liu Jingsheng was charged with "organizing and leading a counter-revolutionary group" and "carrying out counter-revolutionary propaganda and incitement". In December 1994 he was sentenced to 15 years' imprisonment plus an additional four years' deprivation of political rights.

In 1994 a group of people who had attempted to set up the League for the Protection of the Rights of Working People (LPRWP) were arrested in Beijing. According to its provisional charter, the LPRWP was to be a "corporate social body established according to law"

Yuan Hongbing (above) and Zhou Guoqiang (below) were arrested in March 1994 for sponsoring the League for the Protection of the Rights of Working People. Yuan Hongbing, a law lecturer, remains in prison without formal charges. Zhou Guoqiang, a lawyer, was sentenced without trial to three years of "re-education through labour". © Human Rights in China

devoted to protecting the rights of working people. The League's founders proposed, among other things, to establish an information network to promote labour rights as well as a mediation service to help settle labour disputes. Those detained were arrested before the League's charter was submitted on 9 March 1994 to the Ministry of Civil Administration for registration.

Yuan Hongbing, a law lecturer at Beijing University, and Zhou Guoqiang, a lawyer, both sponsors of the LPRWP, were arrested on 2 and 3 March 1994 respectively. Liu Nianchun, another founder of the League, and three other people involved in trying to register the LPRWP were subsequently detained for short periods. In mid-1995 other sponsors of the League remained in prison, including Yuan Hongbing who was being held without charge. Three had been sentenced without trial to terms of "re-education through labour": Zhou Guoqiang and Zhang Lin, a labour activist from Anhui province, to three years, and Liu Huawen, a Christian who had been associated with the group, to two years. All were sentenced on vague accusations of involvement in activities which "infringed the law" or "disturbed public order", without having been formally charged or tried.

Peasants

Information about peasants in China who have had their basic human rights violated is extremely rare. Details are usually not reported outside the victims' villages and few cases have been fully documented. However, many instances of peasants being beaten or illegally detained by local officials came to light in 1993 when widespread rural unrest broke out in several provinces. In Sichuan, Henan, Anhui and eight other provinces, large numbers of impoverished peasants staged angry protests against local levies and officials' abuse of power.

Discontent had grown in many rural areas in the early 1990s in response to the growing financial burden on peasants. Many people were reduced to poverty or driven from their villages in search of work in the cities because of excessive local taxes and fees, the rising cost of fertilizers and fuel, and the government's failure to pay "white IOU notes" (promises of payment issued to peasants for the compulsory sale of part of their crops to the state). Discontent was also fuelled by growing corruption, "green IOU notes" (issued instead of cash for postal remittances sent to peasants by relatives who had migrated to the cities), the growing disparity between rural and urban incomes, and in some areas the requisition of land for building projects for which farmers received little compensation.

In many areas peasants petitioned the authorities against the heavy taxes or staged protests. Some were beaten or jailed as a result. In one of the cases documented by Amnesty International, Hu Hai, a farmer from Liuzhuang county, Henan province, was sentenced in 1991 to three years' imprisonment for peacefully leading villagers to make petitions to the authorities.[15]

Xiang Wenqing was one of at least eight peasants arrested in 1993 in Renshou county, Sichuan province, allegedly for leading a peasant uprising there. Renshou is a low-income area in which many peasants could not pay a new local tax imposed in late 1992. Some had their personal property confiscated in lieu of payment. Protests against the tax accompanied by rioting erupted in January 1993. They were quelled but revived again in May 1993. According to various sources, some of these protests were violent, but it is not clear whether Xiang Wenqing was involved. He is said to have circulated in May documents showing that the tax levy violated central government instructions. His arrest on 5 June and that of other peasants provoked further violent protests which were ended by paramilitary troops. Xiang Wenqing was subsequently sentenced to nine years' imprisonment and others to shorter prison terms.[16] The authorities have not disclosed any information about their trial and their current fate remains unknown.

3

Other targets of repression

Many other people who are seen by the authorities to be stepping out of line are targeted for human rights violations. Some are victims of repressive laws; others fall foul of officials exercising arbitrary power. In China's "autonomous" regions, members of ethnic groups live under the shadow of repressive rules and regulations that deny them the right to express peacefully their national, religious or cultural aspirations and allow officials to flagrantly abuse human rights. The same shadow hangs over people belonging to religious groups that are not authorized by the state. And every single family in China is affected by the birth control policy, which is enforced in ways that encourage coercion and abuse by officials. Such laws and practices contribute to a climate of fear in which no one feels safe.

Tibetans

Gross violations of human rights have intensified in the Tibet Autonomous Region (TAR) since a resurgence of demonstrations and other activities in favour of Tibet's independence began in September 1987.[17] Amnesty International takes no position on the political status of Tibet. Its concerns rest with the authorities' denial of free speech and association in the region, and the persistent pattern of gross violations of other fundamental human rights in connection with the suppression of the nationalist movement.

Thousands of Tibetan nationalists have been arbitrarily detained and many have been tortured. They have been imprisoned for peaceful activities such as displaying the Tibetan national flag, distributing pro-independence posters and leaflets, expressing opposition to Chinese rule in Tibet in private conversations, and possessing audio, visual or written material by or about Tibet's exiled spiritual leader, the Dalai Lama. Many juveniles have been among those imprisoned and tortured. Hundreds of monks and nuns, some of them novices as young as 13, have been jailed for staging small and peaceful demonstrations around the Barkor circuit in Lhasa, during which they shouted pro-independence slogans. Between 1987 and 1989 dozens of demonstrators were killed by the security forces during public protests, some of them in circumstances which amount to extrajudicial executions.[18]

In early March 1989 martial law was declared in Lhasa and remained in force for more than a year. It was imposed during large-scale protests in favour of independence which included violent confrontations with security forces. Over a thousand people were reportedly detained. Official sources acknowledged only 400 arrests and in 1991 reported that 218 Tibetans involved in pro-independence demonstrations had been sentenced by the courts or "sent to receive re-education through labour" between September 1987 and April 1991.

The People's Liberation Army patrolling Lhasa in a truck after the imposition of martial law, March 1989. © TIN

Following the lifting of martial law the authorities imposed new restrictions on public assembly. Arbitrary arrests continued. In early 1995 at least 650 political detainees were being held in Tibet, according to unofficial sources. Most were prisoners of conscience — Buddhist monks and nuns detained solely for their peaceful expression of support for Tibetan independence. Some were held without charge or trial, others were serving long prison terms imposed after unfair trials. Many were reported to have been tortured.

One of the oldest known prisoners of conscience is Lobsang Tsondru, a Buddhist monk and theologian from Drepung monastery near Lhasa. Various sources indicate that he was aged between 77 and 83 when he was arrested in March or April 1990. He was sentenced later to six years' imprisonment for "involvement in illegal separatist activities". He is reported to have been severely beaten by prison guards and lost consciousness in an incident involving several prisoners in April 1991. He was then held in solitary confinement for at least five months. He was reported in 1993 to have heart disease. In July 1994 his case was submitted by the UN Special Rapporteur on torture to the Chinese Government, which simply replied that Lobsang Tsondru was in good health.

Jigme Sangpo, a former primary school teacher now in his sixties, is serving one of the longest sentences imposed on a prisoner of conscience in Tibet. By the time he is due to be released, in 2011, Jigme Sangpo will have spent 28 unbroken years in prison. In 1983, aged 57, he was sentenced to 15 years' imprisonment for "counter-revolutionary propaganda and incitement". In 1988 he received an additional five-year prison sentence for shouting pro-independence slogans in jail. In December 1991 he was reported to have been beaten for shouting slogans during a visit to Drapchi prison by the Swiss Ambassador to China and to have been subsequently held in solitary confinement for at least six weeks. His sentence was again increased, this time by a further eight years. He remains in Drapchi prison. Jigme Sangpo had spent at least 13 years in prison for similar offences before 1980.

In May 1992, 25-year-old Ngawang Choekyi was among several nuns from Toelung Nyen Nunnery who were arrested in Lhasa because they had joined a pro-independence demonstration. She was sentenced to five years' imprisonment and sent to Drapchi prison. In 1993 her sentenced was increased by eight years after she

Jigme Sangpo, a Tibetan prisoner of conscience, will have spent 28 unbroken years in prison by the time he is due for release in 2011. © TIN

and 13 other nuns were convicted of "spreading counter-revolutionary propaganda" for having composed and recorded pro-independence songs in prison.

In recent years discontent has grown in rural areas in Tibet, resulting in an increasing number of protests in villages. This has led to the arbitrary detention of more lay men and women than in previous years, most of them accused of putting up illegal posters, staging demonstrations or organizing underground groups.

In 1994 new security measures were introduced to prevent nationalist demonstrations and limit the scope of religious activities. The sale of photographs of the Dalai Lama was banned, as was possession of them by government employees. CCP members in the TAR and most government officials who were not Party members were told to remove any signs of religion from their homes.

In September 1994 the authorities published new regulations on security, targeted mainly at people engaging in "splittist" (nationalist) activities, which established a new security body to oversee security in all institutions and enterprises, including temples and monasteries. The implementation of these measures apparently provoked protests in monasteries and elsewhere, which were immediately suppressed by the security forces, notably by raids on monasteries and nunneries.

Arrests of monks, nuns and lay people have continued throughout 1995. Many were detained in the TAR and Gansu province after allegedly promoting Tibetan independence. Some were arrested in connection with events organized by the authorities on 1 September to mark the 30th anniversary of the establishment of the TAR. Others detained earlier in the year continue to be held. They include Chadrel Rimpoche, a former abbot of Tashilhunpo monastery, who was arrested in mid-May in connection with a dispute over recognition of a young boy as the reincarnation of the Panchen Lama, the second highest spiritual leader in Tibet. Chadrel Rimpoche is reported to be in poor health.

Muslim ethnic groups

Members of various other ethnic groups have been subjected to human rights violations in connection with demands for political independence, respect for cultural identity or religious freedom. The best documented reports about such violations concern the Xinjiang Autonomous Region. There are other regions in which there is believed to be a similar pattern of abuses but about which information is extremely hard to gather.

Xinjiang is one of the five autonomous regions of the PRC where the officially recognized "national minorities" exercise in theory a degree of self-government. Ethnic Chinese, or Han, form 38 per cent of the Xinjiang population of about 15 million, according to official 1990 census figures. Turkic peoples, including Uighur, Uzbek, Khalkhas and Kazakh, are the main officially recognized "national minorities" and together comprise about 56 per cent of the population. The Turkic peoples of Xinjiang are predominantly Muslim.

Most human rights violations in Xinjiang have been connected to the restriction of religious activities, the repression of nationalist demonstrations and the suppression of underground opposition groups. In recent years, the authorities have reported on several occasions that they had crushed "illegal organizations" in Xinjiang which allegedly aimed to "split the unity of the motherland". Such reports were made in 1990 about groups in Yili, a Kazakh prefecture

in northern Xinjiang, and in Baren, a Uighur rural county in the Akto district, south of Kashgar, in western Xinjiang.

Following violent clashes between demonstrators and the security forces in Baren in April 1990, the authorities imposed a severe crackdown on opposition. Several thousand people were reportedly arrested across Xinjiang. More than 200 people, most of them peasants, were arrested in Baren for involvement in the clashes and many were reportedly tortured. Some were said to have had teeth and limbs broken as a result of beatings in detention and all were reported to be held in extremely harsh conditions.

Amnesty International has received details of 33 Uighur men reported to have been killed or arrested during the Baren incident, including photographs of 31 of them. Eight were reportedly shot dead by the security forces; the 25 others were imprisoned. Of the 25, three were sentenced to death and reportedly taken to Baren town centre and publicly executed; one was sentenced to death with a two-year reprieve; 10 were sentenced to prison terms ranging from 14 years to life; and one received a five-year sentence. At least four of the others detained were still being held without charge or trial in 1993. The fate and whereabouts of the rest is unknown. Those known to have been sentenced are held in various prisons and labour camps in Wusu, Shihezi and Urumqi.

Amnesty International is concerned about allegations that some of those killed were shot as they were fleeing, when they posed no immediate threat of violence. It believes they may have been victims of extrajudicial executions. The organization is also concerned by reports that those jailed were tortured and received heavy sentences after unfair trials. It believes some may be prisoners of conscience.

Amnesty International also has information about some 30 other people who are reported to have been detained or imprisoned in Xinjiang for attempting to exercise fundamental rights or for taking part in protests or underground political groups. Little is known about many of the prisoners in view of the difficulties involved in gathering information. However, corroboration of the arrests has often been provided by official sources.

A man from Xinjiang and a policeman: many people trying to exercise fundamental rights have been victims of human rights violations in Xinjiang.
© *Magnum*

Among such cases is that of Kajikhumar Shabdan (Hajihumaer), an ethnic Kazakh writer and poet. According to official sources, he was detained in July 1987 and later sentenced to 15 years' imprisonment, reportedly for "espionage". Unofficial sources say that he was held on suspicion of belonging to an underground organization in Xinjiang which had links with a nationalist political group in what was then the Kazakhstan Soviet Republic of the USSR. He had published several volumes of a novel, *Crime*, which criticizes the policies towards the region's Turkic peoples implemented by successive administrations in the region. Kajikhumar Shabdan was last reported, in mid-1994, to be serving his sentence at Urumqi No.1 Prison. He was then 70 years old. Amnesty International is concerned that he may be a prisoner of conscience.

Large-scale arrests of Muslim nationalists are also reported to have been carried out in Xinjiang and other areas in the west of China following sporadic unrest since mid-1993. These include mass arrests in Kashgar of people who had reportedly taken part in a public demonstration of grief at the death of a venerated mullah and Islamic scholar in August 1993. Other arrests were made later that year in Kashgar following bombings allegedly carried out by Muslim nationalists.

In October 1993 the authorities crushed two months of anti-Chinese protests by thousands of Muslims in Xining, Qinghai province. As in other incidents, the protests were triggered by the publication of a book which included a picture some Muslims found offensive, but soon turned into nationalist demonstrations. The authorities stormed a mosque which had been occupied for several weeks by the protesters and arrested over a dozen people. They are reported to have been sentenced, but no further information is available.

Religious groups

Zheng Yunsu, the leader of the Jesus Family, a Protestant community in Shandong province, is one of many people who are behind bars simply for practising their religion. He was arrested during a police raid on the community in 1992 and later sentenced to 12

Kajikhumar Shabdan, an ethnic Kazakh writer and poet, was sentenced to 15 years' imprisonment, reportedly for "espionage". He may be a prisoner of conscience. © Xinjiang People's Publishing House

Many leaders and members of the Jesus Family, a Protestant community in Shandong province, have been harassed and imprisoned. The photograph shows the group's houses after their destruction by police in Duoyiguo village, Weishan county, in 1992.

A Christian church in Yongkang, Zhejiang province. All places of worship must be registered with the Chinese authorities. Those involved in religious activities in unregistered places may be punished.

years' imprisonment for "disrupting public order" and "swindling". His four sons and other members of the group were also imprisoned. Amnesty International believes they are prisoners of conscience.

Such persecution of religious groups has followed a substantial religious revival in China over the past 15 years. In the Christian community, much of the expansion has been in religious groups that conduct their activities outside the Protestant and Catholic churches recognized by the government. Many peaceful but unregistered religious gatherings have been raided by police, and those attending have been beaten, threatened or detained. Many of those detained are required to pay heavy fines as a condition for release. Those regarded as "leaders" are usually kept in custody and either sentenced to prison terms or administratively detained without charge or trial.

In January 1994, two national regulations on religious activities came into force. They included some new guarantees to protect human rights, but also consolidated restrictions on religious activities already provided by local regulations. Notably, they banned religious activities which "undermine national unity and social stability", a formulation that leaves room for wide interpretation. They also require that all "places of religious activities" be registered with the authorities according to rules formulated by the government's Religious Affairs Bureau. This means in effect that religious groups that do not have official approval may not obtain registration, and that those involved in religious activities in unregistered places may be detained and punished. Detention and criminal penalties are listed as punishments for violation of the regulations.

Police raids on religious gatherings organized by independent groups have continued during the past year, with hundreds of Protestants and Catholics reportedly detained as a result. More than 200 Christians were reported to have been detained in Xihua county, Henan province, between October 1994 and June 1995, in what appears to have been a new crackdown by local police on unregistered Protestant house-churches. Forty of those arrested in June were still in custody one month later. Most of those detained in previous raids were released after paying heavy fines, ranging from 300 to 1,800 yuan. The latter figure represents one to two years' salary for a farmer in the area. One of the preachers who had

A secret house-church meeting held in Kunming, Yunnan province.

been arrested in October 1994, Ren Ping, was later sentenced without trial to three years of "re-education through labour".

A Christian woman from the area who was interviewed by the *South China Morning Post* stated:

> *"The fines were very heavy. We had to borrow money to pay them. They are arresting us for the money. We are too frightened to stay at home because they could come and pick us up any time. We sleep and worship in the fields."*[19]

Other people arrested for practising their religion include more than 30 Roman Catholics who were arrested in Jiangxi province in April 1995 in connection with the celebration of Easter Sunday Mass on Yi Jia Shan mountain in Chongren county. The mountain has long been used as a place of worship by Roman Catholics from across Jiangxi province. Many of those held in April 1995 were reportedly severely beaten by police at the time of arrest. Most were released after short periods although at least 14, most of them women, were fined 900 yuan. One woman, 18-year-old Rao Yan-ping, was reportedly sentenced to four years in prison on 9 June 1995, and three men received prison terms ranging from two to five years.

Arrests of Christians have continued in various provinces since then. Those held reportedly included 300 people detained in June 1995 after police raids on house-churches in Anhui province. Most were released after paying fines of between 800 and 1,000 yuan, but several house-church leaders reportedly remained in custody in September 1995.

Religious secret societies

Many members of religious secret societies are reported to be serving long prison sentences on conviction of "counter-revolutionary" offences. Many have reportedly been ill-treated in prison.

Traditional secret societies which flourished in China under the old regime were banned as "counter-revolutionary" after 1949 and tens of thousands of their members were jailed or executed. Some of the societies, like the Triads, were involved in organized crime, but many others represented ancient forms of social and economic organization, providing mutual support for particular social groups. Many of them were essentially sectarian religious groups based on traditional beliefs. Dozens of these secret religious societies, such as the *Yi Guan Dao* (Way of Unity), had revived

A group of Christians worshipping in a rural area of Heilongjiang province.

during the late 1970s in various provinces. They were targeted by the authorities and members were arrested. Such arrests have continued in recent years.

Many members of the *Yi Guan Dao* reportedly remain in jail in north China. Some were imprisoned in the 1950s. Others were arrested in the northern provinces of Shanxi, Shaanxi and Gansu and other places between 1981 and 1983. They were reportedly involved only in spreading the doctrine of the society. They were summarily tried and sentenced at the height of an "anti-crime" campaign launched in August 1983 that resulted in thousands of summary executions. Some were sentenced to death and others were sentenced to long terms of imprisonment.

One of those who received a heavy sentence is Lei Yuesheng, who lived in Jijiawan Brigade, Huaxu commune, Lantian county in Shaanxi province. In 1981, when aged 25, he was arrested and sentenced to a prison term together with several other people accused of carrying out "counter-revolutionary" activities on behalf of the *Yi Guan Dao*. While in prison in 1983, Lei Yuesheng and others allegedly "refused to reform their behaviour" and "secretly carried out their activities" from prison. On 9 October 1983 the Weinan county People's Court deemed such activities to be part of a "reactionary plot to stir up rumour and alarm among the masses". It sentenced Lei Yuesheng and four other *Yi Guan Dao* prisoners to death, and another to death with a two-year reprieve. The sentences were upheld by the Shaanxi High People's Court on 29 October 1983. In December that year, the Supreme People's Court confirmed all the sentences except the death sentence on Lei Yuesheng, which was changed to death with a two-year reprieve. Four members of the group were executed. The fate of Lei Yuesheng and of another man, Luo Sanxing, who also received a suspended death sentence, remains unknown.

Amnesty International has the names and details of many other *Yi Guan Dao* members jailed in the early 1980s. Former prisoners told Amnesty International that many were still imprisoned in Shaanxi province in the early 1990s. This was confirmed in 1994 by former *Yi Guan Dao* prisoners released after more than 40 years in jail in Shaanxi province. They said that fewer than a hundred of the prisoners remained alive in Weinan prison (Shaanxi provincial Prison No. 2), but that several hundred who had been imprisoned in the 1950s remained in Fuping prison (Shaanxi provincial Prison No. 1). They spoke of harsh prison conditions and frequent beating by guards and other prisoners. They said that over the years hundreds of prisoners had died of old age or as a result of ill-treatment and neglect.[20]

Human rights violations resulting from the birth control policy

Many people, especially women, have suffered violations of their most fundamental rights as a result of China's birth control policy.[21] Birth control has been compulsory since 1979. The government argues that population control is essential for China's modernization and food security. Government demographers have set a target for the stabilization of the population at 1.3 billion by the year 2000, which they claim can only be achieved through "strict measures".

The policy involves controlling the age of marriage and the timing and number of children for each couple. Women must have official permission to bear children. Birth control is enforced

A poster extolling the virtues of the "one-child family" in Fujian province.
© *Sean Sprague/Panos*

through quotas allocated to each work or social unit (such as school, factory or village), which fix the number of children that may be born annually. In most regions, urban couples may have only one child unless their child is disabled, while rural couples may have a second if the first is a girl. A third child is "prohibited" according to most available regulations. Abortions are mandatory for unmarried women as well as for migrant women who do not return to their home region. Local party officials (cadres) have always monitored the system, but since 1991 they have been held directly responsible for its implementation through "target management responsibility contracts". Cadres may face penalties if they fail to keep within quotas.

The authorities in Beijing initially exempted ethnic groups with populations of less than 10 million from the one-child policy and even from family planning more generally. It is clear, however, that controls have been applied to these groups for many years, including the more stringent sanctions for urban residents. There have also been reports since 1988 of controls extending to enforcement of one-child families, in particular for state employees. Currently, as with the rest of the population, specific regulations and their implementation are decided by "Autonomous Regions and Provinces where the minorities reside".

Couples who have a child "above the quota" are subject to sanctions, including heavy fines. In rural areas, there have been reports of the demolition of the houses of people who failed to pay fines. State employees may be dismissed or demoted. Psychological intimidation and harassment are also commonly used to "persuade" pregnant women to have an abortion. Groups of family planning officials may visit them at night to this end. In the face of such pressure, women facing unwanted abortions or sterilization are likely to feel they have no option but to comply.

Amnesty International takes no position on the official birth control policy in China, but is concerned about the human rights violations which result from it. It is concerned at reports that forced abortion and sterilization have been carried out by or at the instigation of people acting in an official capacity, such as family planning officials, against women who are detained or forcibly taken from their homes to have the operation. Amnesty International considers that in these circumstances such actions amount to torture or cruel, inhuman and degrading treatment.

The use of forcible measures is indicated in official family planning reports and regulations, and in Chinese press reports. Amnesty International has also received testimony from former family planning officials as well as individuals who were ill-treated. A former family planning official described to Amnesty International the threat of violence used to implement the policy:

> *"Several times I have witnessed how women who were five to seven months pregnant were protected by their neighbours and relatives, some of whom used tools against us. Mostly the police only had to show their weapons to scare them off. Sometimes they had to shoot in the air. In only one case did I see them shoot at hands and feet. Sometimes we had to use handcuffs."*

Several family planning officials, who worked in Liaoning and Fujian provinces from the mid-1980s to the mid-1990s and are now in exile, have reported that they detained women who were pregnant with "out of plan children" in storerooms or offices for as long as they resisted having an abortion. This could last several days. One official reported being able to transfer such women to the local detention centre for up to two months if they remained intransigent. Once a woman relented, the official would escort her to the local hospital and wait until a doctor had signed a statement that the abortion had been carried out. Unless the woman was considered too weak, it was normal for her to be sterilized straight after the abortion.

A man from Guangdong province described to Amnesty International how he and his wife had suffered under the birth control policy. The couple had their first child in 1982 and were subsequently denied permission to have another. In 1987 the authorities discovered that the wife was pregnant and forced her to have an abortion. In 1991 she became pregnant again and to conceal it, the couple moved to live with relatives in another village. In September that year local militia and family planning officials from the city of Foshan surrounded the village in the middle of the night and searched all the houses. They forced pregnant women into trucks and drove them to hospital. The man's wife gave birth on the journey and a doctor at the hospital reportedly killed the baby with an injection. The other women had forced abortions.

The implementation of the birth control policy has also resulted in the arbitrary detention and ill-treatment of relatives of those attempting to avoid abortion or sterilization. Significantly, the Supreme People's Court felt the need specifically to outlaw the taking of hostages by government officials in a directive in 1990. However, the practice continues, as shown by a series of reports since late 1992 from Hebei Province.

Villagers in Fengjiazhuang and Longtiangou in Lingzhou county, Hebei province, alleged they were targeted in a birth control campaign initiated in early 1994 under the slogan "better to have more graves than more than one child". Ninety per cent of residents in the villages are Roman Catholic. Among those targeted was an unmarried woman. She had adopted one of her brother's children after he and his wife had fled their village fearing sterilization as they had four children. The woman was detained several times, including once in early November 1994 when she was held for seven days in an attempt to force her brother and his wife to return and pay more fines. She was taken to the county government office and locked in a basement room with 12 to 13 other women and men. She was reportedly blindfolded, stripped naked, with her hands tied behind her back, and beaten with an electric baton. Several of those detained with her were suspended above the ground and beaten, and some were detained for several weeks.

Despite assurances from the State Family Planning Commission that "coercion is not permitted", Amnesty International has been unable to find any instance of sanctions imposed on officials who perpetrated such violations. In the light of the information available about serious human rights violations resulting from the enforcement of the birth control policy, Amnesty International calls on the Chinese Government to include in relevant regulations explicit and unequivocal prohibition of coercive methods which result in such violations. It also calls on the authorities to take effective measures to ensure that officials who perpetrate, encourage or condone such human rights violations during birth control enforcement are brought to justice.

4

Torture and impunity

"When we arrived at the police station, the tall thin one boxed my ears five or six times, then hit me with his electric truncheon, forcing me to the floor. Then they put handcuffs on me... After several blows to my head and face I saw stars and fell to the floor. They pulled me to my feet by my hair and continued the beating. I reckon he hit me with about 30 blows. Another fat policeman kicked my legs, an older man stood by, watching. By now, I was nauseous and wanting to vomit... At last I collapsed on the floor and could not struggle. Then another policeman came over and kicked me in the groin... They went on kicking my stomach and groin. My groin was unbearably painful and I tried to protect it with my hands. They pulled me by the hair and forced me to squat. By now my hands had lost almost all feeling..."[22]

This is the testimony of Yan Zhengxue, a 50-year-old painter and deputy of a local People's Congress in Zhejiang province. He was detained after police had been called following an argument with a bus conductor in Beijing on 2 July 1993. Even though he was not suspected of a crime, he was taken to the Haidian district police station where the police beat him without a word of explanation. Eventually, late at night, Yan Zhengxue was pushed out of the police station, almost unconscious. A passer-by took him to the Xiyuan hospital, which recorded multiple bruising and abrasions to his back, head, hands, shoulders and groin. Yan Zhengxue filed a suit against his attackers, but, in retribution, the police framed him on a misdemeanour and he was sent to a labour camp (see Chapter 1).

Yan Zhengxue's testimony and similar reports from many other sources are a grim reminder that torture is routinely practised in

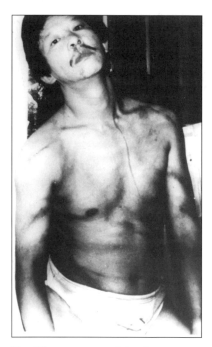

Yan Zhengxue, a painter from Beijing, was severely beaten on the head and kicked in the stomach and groin by police. This picture was taken shortly after he was released from hospital. © Open Magazine

many parts of China, despite the government's declared opposition to its use. The reports show that safeguards against torture in Chinese law are manifestly inadequate and that anyone arrested or detained is vulnerable to such treatment. They indicate that the government's approach to investigating and prosecuting cases of reported torture is arbitrary and inconsistent, offering impunity to many torturers. They also show that China is failing to live up to its obligations as a State Party to the UN Convention against Torture and Other Cruel, Inhuman or Degrading Treatment or Punishment (Convention against Torture).

Torture occurs not just as an incidental breach of the law, as the Chinese authorities claim, but as a result of institutionalized practices and official policies. Acknowledgement of "guilt" is as much a part of the penal system as it is of the criminal process, and efforts to compel it lead to many abuses. The authorities, however, acknowledge only some of the abuses.

"Torture to extract confessions" is explicitly prohibited by Chinese law. The authorities investigate some cases and prosecute some perpetrators. In 1994, for instance, they reported that 409 cases of "torture to extract confessions" were investigated.[23] But the law is enforced in an arbitrary way. For every case investigated, there are countless others which are ignored or covered up by officials. And for certain categories of "offenders", the law offers no protection at all: torture and ill-treatment are used as instruments of repressive state policies.

While it is difficult to assess the extent of torture quantitatively, there is evidence to show that its use is widespread, systemic and far higher than suggested by official statistics. In the past six years, Amnesty International has received allegations of torture and ill-treatment of prisoners in penal institutions and detention centres in practically all regions of China, including in Beijing, Shanghai and Tianjin municipalities, in the Tibet, Xinjiang and Inner Mongolia autonomous regions, and in Liaoning, Shaanxi, Shanxi, Hebei, Henan, Anhui, Hubei, Hunan, Jiangsu, Fujian, Guangdong, Gansu and other provinces. The patterns of torture and ill-treatment described by unofficial sources are confirmed by reports in the Chinese press.

Patterns of torture

Torture is inflicted on political and common criminal prisoners alike. Anyone is at risk if they cross the authorities. People who were not suspected of any crime have been tortured because they became involved in disputes with police and other officials, or because they attempted to defend their rights. The victims come from all walks of life and include children and the elderly. Those most vulnerable are the less educated or less privileged, such as peasants, the unemployed and vagrants.

The torturers are usually police officers belonging to the public security agencies, or personnel from other security and judicial agencies, such as prison officials. Local CCP or government officials, judges and procurators have also been involved in torture. "Cell bosses" or "prison trustees" — prisoners who are entrusted by prison officials to supervise other prisoners — are often allowed to abuse prisoners at will and carry out the wardens' instructions to "teach a lesson" to "resistant" prisoners. Their cooperation is rewarded by privileges or even a reduction of sentence. Former prisoners say the system of "cell bosses" allows prison officials to deny responsibility if a prisoner makes a complaint, suffers injury or dies as a result of ill-treatment. In such cases, prison officials

THE SAFETY ELECTRONIC EQUIPMENT BRANCH FACTORY OF
TIANJIN BOHAI RADIO WORKS

Instruments of torture:
(above) *electric batons*
and (left) *thumb cuffs.*

usually blame a fight between prisoners, or support the perpetrators' claims that the victim's injuries were self-inflicted.

The most common forms of torture include severe beatings with fists or a variety of instruments, whipping, kicking, the use of electric batons which give powerful electric shocks, the use of handcuffs or leg-irons in ways that cause intense pain, and suspension by the arms, often combined with beatings. Some torture methods have resulted in death.

Other common forms of torture or cruel, inhuman or degrading treatment include incarceration in tiny or dark cells without heat, ventilation or sanitation; handcuffing for prolonged periods; exposure to intense cold or heat; deprivation of food or sleep; and being made to sit or stand without moving for long periods. Some of these methods are applied simultaneously. In many labour camps and prison factories, prisoners' work and living conditions amount in themselves to cruel, inhuman and degrading treatment, with prisoners being required to carry out heavy labour for long hours and facing punishment if they do not fulfil work quotas.

In some places of detention, particularly cruel methods of torture have been reported. For example, during the early 1990s some female and male prisoners in Guangzhou No.1 Detention Centre, known as Huanghua prison, Guangdong province, were reportedly shackled on the "tiger bed" (*laohu chuang*). The device consists of a wooden door laid flat on short legs with handcuffs at the four corners. Prisoners are attached to the board with their arms and legs spread out and handcuffed at the corners. A hole in the centre of the board allows evacuation of urine and excrement. A similar device, known as the "shackle board", was also reportedly used during the same period in several detention centres in Hunan province, including the Hunan provincial No.3 Prison in Lingling and the Changsha No.1 Detention Centre. Some prisoners were reportedly attached to the shackle board for weeks on end and became mentally disturbed as a result. It is not known whether the devices are still used.

Torture of criminal suspects

Criminal suspects are frequently tortured and ill-treated during preliminary or pre-trial detention in police stations or detention centres in order to intimidate them, force them to give information about themselves or others, or coerce confessions. Abuse may continue for weeks or months as investigators try to gather from detainees sufficient "evidence" to initiate an indictment and proceed with trial.

Among many cases reported in the past year were those of four girls aged under 16 and two young men who were tortured by a Public Security section chief intent on making them "confess" to "hooligan and promiscuous behaviour". Detained in Fuxin, Liaoning province, in early 1995, they were repeatedly hit, kicked and given shocks with an electric baton. They were only released after their families had paid 5,000 yuan (about US$ 580) to the section chief. In Taoyuan county, Hunan province, three women working for a private restaurant were tortured in March 1995 by a police sub-station chief to make them "confess" to prostitution. Their hands were tied behind their back and they were made to squat. They were then beaten and lashed with a stick for several hours. Their employer and another man were later detained, beaten and fined more than 10,000 yuan.[24]

Such incidents are common, but few are ever reported in the Chinese press. A former police officer from Shanghai told Amnesty International a few years ago that there were "hundreds" of unacknowledged cases of torture and ill-treatment in the city for every one that was officially investigated. A former procuracy employee from Wuhan, Hubei province, described a climate in which the beating of "hooligans" at the city's police stations was considered so normal that it did not occur to the victims to complain and procurators did not think it worth investigating.

In many instances, torture and ill-treatment have resulted in death. While official statistics on the number of deaths in custody are not published, Amnesty International has recorded in the past few years several dozen deaths as a result of torture that have been reported in the Chinese press. These are believed to represent only a fraction of the true total. Press reports focus almost entirely on people who were tortured to death shortly after arrest, usually in police stations. Most involve cases in which the authorities have eventually taken action to bring the perpetrators to justice. The press has hardly ever reported deaths in penal institutions or torture for reasons other than "to extract confessions", and usually remains silent about the treatment of political prisoners.

The press reports nevertheless show that deaths as a result of torture are not rare. For instance, the *Henan Legal Daily* of 7 October 1993 stated that 41 prisoners and "innocent" suspects had died as a result of torture during interrogation between 1990 and 1992 in Henan province alone.[25] The newspaper noted that torture methods had become more cruel, citing cases in which victims were tied and hung up, had boiling water poured over them, were hit with bottles, burned with cigarettes, whipped with leather or plastic belts, or had electric prods placed on their genitals.[26] Other deaths owing to torture reported in 1993 included cases in Anhui, Guangdong, Gansu, Sichuan and Shanxi provinces, and eight cases in an unidentified province reported by the *Shenzhen Legal Daily* in August. Among the victims were an 11-year-old boy and a disabled man.

Liang Rihua was arrested on 17 May 1993 on suspicion of stealing chickens. He was tortured to death by police determined that he should confess to the alleged crime. According to a newspaper report, several police officers from the Tang Peng police station in Lianjiang county, Guangdong province, handcuffed Liang Rihua's hands behind his back, tied an electric wire to the handcuffs and suspended him by the wire from a window frame with his feet barely touching the ground. A few hours later he was dead. Following examination by legal and medical experts, Liang Rihua's death was found to have been caused by "prolonged suspension by the arms and beating".[27] A senior officer of the Tang Peng police unit was reported to have been arrested in September 1993 for directing the torture of Liang Rihua, but no further developments are known to Amnesty International.

Yang Hongquan was accused of stealing chickens and shoes in a village in Mianzhu county, Sichuan province, in January 1994. Within three hours of his detention he had been tortured to death by a police officer and other people, while the local police chief directed his "interrogation".[28] In another case, Shen Fengqi, a school teacher in Changzhi city, Shanxi province, died in July 1994 after 17 days in detention during which he was tortured by five police officers, including the city's police chief. He had been illegally detained on a false accusation that he had prompted another man to make crank telephone calls to the police chief. His wife, brother and a fellow teacher were also illegally detained and beaten by police.[29]

Cases of criminal suspects tortured to death have also been reported by unofficial sources, but few can be checked or verified. One such report received by Amnesty International concerned an 18-year-old boy, Shi Shufei, who was allegedly tortured to death by police in the Public Security Bureau Detention Centre in Dandong city, Liaoning province. According to the report, he had been arrested in May 1993 on suspicion of stealing a necklace from a policeman's relative. He was then tortured by police in a bid to extort money from him or his family. He reportedly died in the detention centre in November 1993, following which his family appealed in vain to the authorities to investigate the case. The press was not interested either, telling the family that there were "legal restrictions on news reporting".

Torture of political detainees

Torture is often used as an instrument of political repression. While the authorities might in some instances bring to justice those who torture common criminal suspects, they never do so in political cases. Dissidents with a high international profile may enjoy some protection, but for ordinary members of groups targeted by the state, torture is an everyday risk.

Hundreds of political detainees were tortured in the months following the government's crackdown on the 1989 pro-democracy movement. For example, Gao Xu, a computer student, was reported to have been severely beaten after his arrest in Beijing on 4 June 1989 as well as when he was transferred to the Taiyuan city Detention Centre in Shanxi province. In 1993 he was reportedly nearly blind in one eye and suffering constant severe headaches as a result of the torture. Zhou Min, a worker arrested during the June 1989 crackdown in Changsha, Hunan province, was reportedly beaten and tortured with electric batons repeatedly for a year at the Changsha No.1 Detention Centre, becoming mentally disturbed as a result.

Torture of political suspects has continued to be reported since 1989. Among many cases were those of Sun Liyong, a former cadre, and four other people arrested in Beijing in May 1991 for publishing and circulating a magazine criticizing the government. They were said to have been repeatedly beaten during an 18-month period while held incommunicado at Qincheng prison.[30] Li Guotao, a human rights activist in Shanghai (see Chapter 2), was reportedly severely beaten by police during interrogation while briefly detained in 1993.

In Tibet, people are frequently tortured and ill-treated when held on suspicion of supporting Tibetan independence or during police raids on monasteries. In January 1995, for example, 20-year-old Pasang and 22-year-old Ngodrup, two monks from the Jokhang temple in Lhasa, were reportedly beaten while held in police custody for three days. Pasang was said to have been beaten so badly that he could not stand up and had severe back pain after his release. In another case, in a Tibetan area in Xiahe county, Gansu province, Jigme Gyatso was allegedly tortured by police in May 1995 after he had been detained on suspicion of supporting the Tibetan independence movement. He was reportedly beaten until he was unable to move his hands and feet, possibly suffering brain damage. His family had to pay money to the police as a condition of his release.

Tibetan children are also reported to have been tortured. In one of several testimonies received by Amnesty International, a teenager said that he and five other youths, including one aged 13, were kicked and beaten with belts by police officers when they were arrested in December 1993 for singing nationalist songs while walking in the Barkor area in central Lhasa. After being taken to a police station, the youths were forced to remove most of their clothes and were

Ngodrup, a 22-year-old monk from the Jokhang temple in Lhasa, before his arrest. He was reportedly beaten in police custody. Torture and ill-treatment are frequently reported in Tibet. © TIN

beaten with a whip made of wires. Many other incidents of torture and police brutality against Tibetans have been documented by Amnesty International during the past year.[31]

Torture and ill-treatment are also reported to be routine during police raids on unapproved religious meetings. In February 1995 Li Dexian, an evangelist from Guangzhou, was about to address a house-church meeting in Beixing township, near Huadu city in Guangdong, when police officers arrived. According to reports, they kicked him in the groin in front of the congregation, then took him to the police station where he was beaten with a heavy pole, jumped on and kicked by police officers until he vomited blood. The police officers reportedly told him that they had been given instructions from "higher up" to take action against "this form of religion".[32] One month later, police launched another raid on the monthly house-church meeting in Beixing township and again beat Li Dexian. The incident was witnessed by a visiting Australian missionary. Numerous other similar incidents, affecting hundreds of people, have been reported in recent years (see also Chapter 3).

Zheng Musheng, a farmer and house-church Christian from Dongkou county in Hunan province, died in detention in January 1994 apparently as a result of torture. He was reportedly accused of "swindling people and seriously disturbing public order by spreading rumours and fallacies". Unofficial sources say that he was detained because of his religious beliefs. According to several reports, Zheng Musheng was taken to the Shanmen police station in Dongkou county, where he was tortured to make him "confess his crimes". The following day he was reportedly transferred to the Dongkou county Public Security office, where he died. Police officials later told his family that he had died in custody after being beaten and seriously injured by 13 prison inmates. There was no inquest.

Zheng Musheng's family was only notified of his death eight days after he died. They were allowed to see his body on 17 January — 11 days after his death. They said there were deep rope burns on his ankles, indicating he had been tied up, and multiple stab wounds on his body. These injuries were inconsistent with the police claim that he had been beaten by prison inmates. His body was cremated on 19 January, even though Zheng Musheng's widow, Yin Dongxiu, had refused to sign the official document authorizing cremation. She was reportedly offered a large sum of money by the Shanmen and Dongkou police for signing the document, but refused. In May 1994 Yin Dongxiu filed a suit against local and county police officials for mounting a cover-up to conceal the circumstances of her husband's murder. Since then she is reported to have been interrogated by police many times, her house has been ransacked and she has been kept under heavy police surveillance. Meanwhile her legal case has reportedly made little progress. While a growing number of people have brought similar suits against officials in recent years, many remain silent for fear of retaliation or because they think they have no chance of being heard.

Torture and ill-treatment in penal institutions

Torture and ill-treatment of prisoners in China's penal institutions largely result from the official penal policy. "Acknowledgement of guilt" and forced labour are fundamental elements of the reform of "criminals". The application of these principles creates an environment in which abuses of prisoners are almost inevitable.

In many prisons and labour camps, prisoners are expected to conform to standards of behaviour which involve total obedience, however arbitrary the orders they receive. They are frequently humiliated and subjected to punishments which amount to torture or cruel, inhuman or degrading treatment. This may happen if they complain, do not fulfil work quotas, disobey orders or infringe regulations. Such punishments are usually imposed on the grounds that the prisoners have a "bad attitude" or "resist reform". In addition, many prisoners receive inadequate food and fall ill, and are then denied adequate medical care.

Political prisoners held at the Lingyuan No. 2 Labour-Reform Detachment in Liaoning province claimed that they were repeatedly tortured there in 1991 and 1992. According to their account, the abuses started in May 1991 when 11 newly arrived political prisoners refused to acknowledge that they were "criminals", as required by the prison authorities. All were severely beaten and four of them were sent to the "correction unit". There, the four prisoners were stripped naked, held down on the floor and repeatedly given shocks with high-voltage electric batons to their head, neck, shoulders, armpits, stomach and the inside of the legs. When the electric baton used against one of the prisoners, Tang Yuanjuan, ran out of power, he was kicked by a guard and two of his ribs were broken. Another prisoner, Leng Wanbao, had an electric baton forced into his mouth because he remained silent. Similar incidents took place in the following months.[33]

At Hanyang prison, Hubei province, political prisoners have alleged that they were frequently beaten and abused in other ways by prison officers and "trustees". In an appeal dated March 1993, they gave a detailed account of several incidents of torture,[34] including the following one:

> "... The torture did not end there... Prison officers and workers in the brigade went to the solitary confinement cells and inflicted more beatings on Lin Zhiyong and Feng Haiguang, who were in extremely poor health but still refused to submit. Lin's legs were whipped constantly for two hours. This caused him to have enormous difficulties in walking for a long time afterwards. Feng Haiguang was subjected to two more beatings, where police electric whips and electric batons were used. He was tortured for more than three hours each time. During the first beating he sustained over 30 separate wounds and serious swelling and bruising. On the second occasion, they whipped the small of his back and hips, causing his whole back to turn purplish-brown. Three weeks later his wounds had not yet healed..."

In Tibet, political prisoners held at Drapchi prison in Lhasa have been severely beaten, shackled, held for long periods in solitary confinement and tortured or ill-treated in other ways to punish them for expressing their views. In 1991, for example, two prisoners who attempted to hand a petition to US diplomats visiting Drapchi prison were reportedly severely beaten and placed in solitary confinement. Five other prisoners who subsequently protested at the two prisoners' treatment were themselves beaten and had their hands and feet chained before being transferred to another prison. Sixteen prisoners, who in turn protested against the transfer, were also reportedly beaten and punished. One of them was Lobsang Tsondru, a monk aged in his seventies at the time (see Chapter 3).[35]

In a more recent case, Lodroe Gyatso, who is serving 15 years' imprisonment for murder, was reportedly beaten and placed in an isolation cell in Drapchi prison on 4 March 1995. According to reports, he was being punished for shouting pro-independence slogans and attempting to circulate political literature in the prison.

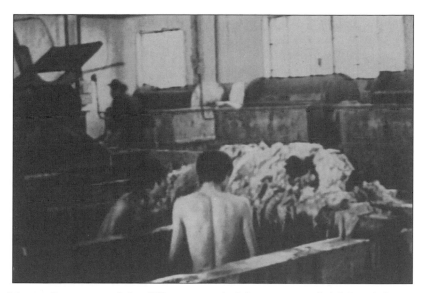

Many prisoners complain of ill-treatment in labour camps. The photograph shows naked prisoners working inside vats of toxic chemicals used for tanning sheepskins in Xining, Qinghai province, in 1991.

He was later given an additional prison term of six years on charges of "instigating unrest to overthrow the government and split the motherland". Many other cases of torture in Tibet have been described by Amnesty International in earlier documents[36] (see also Chapter 3).

Across China many prisoners claim they are beaten when they cannot perform the required work or protest about long hours of work. Prisoners held at a labour camp in Nuomuhong, Qinghai province, reportedly said they were treated like slaves, working for up to 12 hours nearly every day of the year and being beaten if they complained.[37] Zhu Mei (also known as Sha Zhumei), a 72-year-old retired primary school teacher jailed in 1991 at Shanghai municipality's main prison, was reportedly beaten by prison guards on several occasions for failing to finish the work required of her. One of her knees was broken during the beatings, which left her unable to walk. Zhang Lin, a labour activist detained at the Nanhu labour camp in Anhui province, claimed in a letter smuggled out of the camp in late 1994 that, because constant pain in his hands and feet prevented him from working, a guard had repeatedly punched and kicked him and given him shocks with an electric baton. Tong Yi,

LEICESTERSHIRE LIBRARIES & INFORMATION SERVICE
REFERENCE & INFORMATION LIBRARY HUMANITIES

formerly assistant to leading dissident Wei Jingsheng (see Chapter 1), said in January 1995 that she had been repeatedly beaten by two camp "trustees" at the Hewan labour camp in Wuhan, Hubei province. This happened shortly after Tong Yi had complained to the camp authorities about her long hours of work. She said that the day after she complained to camp officials about the beatings, she was again beaten, this time by more than 10 women prisoners. Qin Yongmin, a male prisoner of conscience also held in the Hewan labour camp, described in 1994 the intimidation and abuse of both criminal and political prisoners in the camp.

Chen Pokong, a pro-democracy activist held at the Guangzhou No.1 Re-education Through Labour Centre in Hua county, Guangdong province, claimed in a letter smuggled out of the camp in 1994 that prisoners were frequently abused and forced to work for as long as 14 hours a day; they worked in a stone quarry during the day and made artificial flowers at night. He said:

"Inmates who labour slightly slower are brutally beaten and misused by supervisors and team leaders (themselves inmates). Inmates are often beaten until they are blood-stained all over, collapse or lose consciousness."[38]

Other accounts of torture and ill-treatment of both criminal and political prisoners have been given to Amnesty International in the past few years by former prisoners who had been jailed in prisons or labour camps in various places, including in Beijing and Shanghai, and in Hebei, Hunan, Shanxi and Shaanxi provinces. For example, a former prisoner who was jailed at Shaanxi Prison No.1 in Fuping in 1992 described the prison as "a hell", with prisoners in all categories suffering beatings from guards and similar brutalities and rapes by "cell bosses". He also said that prisoners were given a starvation diet and many had died or committed suicide as a result of the conditions and ill-treatment.

Torture and ill-treatment lead to the death of an untold number of prisoners. Among many cases reported to Amnesty International are those of four young Tibetan nuns who were allegedly ill-treated and died between 1992 and 1995.[39] One of them, Phuntsog Yangkyi, aged 20, was serving a five-year sentence in Drapchi prison for taking part in a pro-independence demonstration in Lhasa in February 1992. According to unofficial sources, she was beaten by prison guards after she and other nuns sang nationalist songs in the prison on 11 February 1994. She apparently lost consciousness after medical staff in the prison gave her medication because she was "speaking uncontrollably". She was transferred in late May or early June 1994 to the police hospital in Lhasa, where she died on 4 June. No independent medical investigation into the cause of her death was reported to have taken place before her burial.

In July 1994 her case was submitted by the UN Special Rapporteur on torture to the Chinese Government. The government replied that the prison administration had discovered in May 1994 that Phuntsog Yangkyi had a tuberculoma and had sent her to hospital. They said that after her death the prison arranged for her remains to be buried in accordance with Tibetan custom. Amnesty International subsequently called on the Chinese authorities to launch an inquiry into the circumstances of her death; no reply was received.

The Chinese authorities have erected a wall of silence around torture and ill-treatment in penal institutions. But the reports which emerge, some of which are described here, show that such practices are widespread and systemic. The authorities' silence and failure to take action to curb

Phuntsog Yangkyi, a 20-year-old Tibetan nun who had been jailed for peaceful pro-independence activities, died in a prison hospital in June 1994 after apparently being beaten by guards. © TIN

77

such abuses amount to official acquiescence in this massive violation of human rights.

Why torture continues

Torture continues in China because of inadequate legislation, the lack of legal guarantees for prisoners' rights and the impunity extended to many torturers. The patterns of torture across China and the authorities' failure to introduce effective measures to combat it or acknowledge and impartially investigate torture allegations suggest that torture often results from institutionalized practices and official policies.

By allowing torture to continue, China is failing to live up to its international responsibilities as a signatory to the Convention against Torture. As a State Party, China is accountable to the UN committee of experts — the Committee Against Torture (CAT) — which monitors implementation of the Convention. When China submitted its first report to the CAT in December 1989, the experts found it inadequate and asked for an additional report. This was submitted in late 1992. It stated that over the years, particularly since China had ratified the Convention in 1988, it had adopted "effective" legislative, judicial, administrative and other measures to "rigorously forbid all acts of torture and guarantee that the rights of the person and the democratic rights of citizens are not violated". The reality, however, is that not all acts of torture are forbidden by law. Furthermore, no fundamental preventive measures have been taken to protect prisoners against torture since the 1980 Criminal Law outlawed some forms of torture. Further laws have introduced a mechanism for seeking compensation, but still the most basic safeguards to prevent torture and ill-treatment, such as early access to lawyers, are lacking. The ineffectiveness of the measures taken by the government is demonstrated by the continuing high incidence of torture in China.

Article 2 of the Convention requires States Parties to take effective measures to prevent torture, not simply to forbid it. Amnesty International believes that such measures should include a fundamental review by the Chinese authorities of the laws and practices which foster the use of torture in China.[40]

Inadequate legislation

Under the Convention against Torture, China is legally bound to criminalize all acts of torture. Torture includes any severe physical or mental pain inflicted for purposes such as obtaining confessions or punishing, intimidating or coercing a person for any reason. The Convention also says that punishments for torture should reflect "their grave nature". Chinese law manifestly fails to meet these obligations.

China's Criminal Law provides punishments for two specific offences involving torture or ill-treatment of prisoners by state officials — "torture to coerce a statement" (Article 136) and "corporal punishment and abuse" (Article 189). In addition, Article 143, which prohibits illegal detention, provides for heavier punishments in cases where victims of illegal detention are ill-treated. These provisions, however, do not punish all acts of torture and ill-treatment, as defined in the Convention against Torture. They do not punish the use of torture to punish, intimidate or coerce a person for any reason. Furthermore, they only prohibit ill-treatment in a number of limited circumstances and only provide for light punishments.

Article 136 of the Criminal Law permits punishments ranging from "criminal detention" to three years' imprisonment in ordinary cases, and from three to seven years' imprisonment if torture has caused serious injury or disability, or more if it causes death. The minimum punishment, "criminal detention", consists of between 15 days' and six months' detention (Article 37). The availability of light punishments for serious acts of torture is well known to police and prison officials and reinforces the sense of impunity given by the knowledge that few torturers are ever brought to justice.

"Corporal punishment and abuse" of prisoners (Article 189) is not considered by Chinese law to be a crime of the same nature and gravity as "torture to coerce a statement". It is not part of the section of the Criminal Law dealing with "crimes of infringing upon the rights of the person and the democratic rights of citizens". Instead, it comes under a section dealing with "crimes of dereliction of duty" by state officials.

Article 189 is applicable specifically to judicial personnel who "violate laws and regulations on prison management" by subjecting prisoners to corporal punishment and abuse. In other words, this applies only to state personnel in penal institutions and thus excludes ill-treatment inflicted on detainees in other places of detention. Furthermore, prison regulations allow the imposition of certain punishments, such as the prolonged use of handcuffs and leg-irons, even though such measures are regarded as constituting ill-treatment and are prohibited under international standards. As a result, such practices do not come under the scope of Article 189. Article 189 also provides that "corporal punishment and abuse" are punishable only "when the circumstances are serious". The law does not specify what circumstances are considered serious, so some perpetrators may escape prosecution. As in Article 136, the minimum punishment is "criminal detention".

No basic safeguards for prisoners' rights

People are totally helpless once they are taken into police custody. They can be held incommunicado for months after arrest

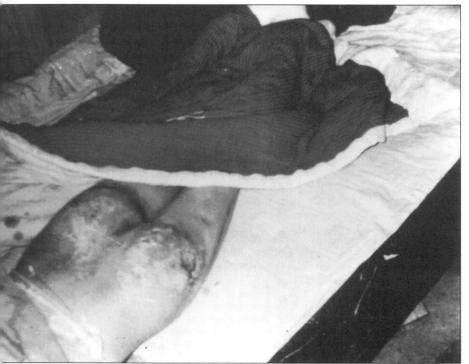

The marks of torture are clearly visible on this victim, beaten during a police raid on a religious meeting in the village of Taoyuan, Shaanxi province, in April 1993.

and are at the mercy of their jailers. Chinese law includes none of the most basic safeguards required by international standards to protect prisoners against torture and ill-treatment, such as the right of prompt and regular access to lawyers, doctors, judges and relatives.

In fact, the law effectively allows the police arbitrarily to hold people in custody without contact with the outside world for weeks or months, even years, if they so wish. It guarantees access to lawyers only when people are prosecuted under the Criminal Law and then only once the procedure for trial has started, usually several months after arrest. Those who are administratively detained have no access to a lawyer or judicial authority unless they appeal.

Family visits are usually granted only after a prisoner has been tried and sentenced or "assigned" a term of administrative detention. They are considered a privilege rather than a right and can therefore be denied. When they are allowed, they take place once a month in the presence of prison guards. All mail is censored. Prisoners can therefore be tortured or ill-treated without anyone outside the prison finding out.

Impunity

Under the Convention against Torture, China is obliged to investigate whenever there are reasonable grounds to believe torture has taken place (Article 12) and to prosecute those responsible (Article 7). However, few judicial investigations into torture allegations.are instigated by the Chinese authorities compared with the high incidence of torture that is reported. Moreover, the climate of impunity is encouraged by frequent cover-ups by the authorities.

The Chinese authorities do not publish statistics about the number of torturers who are prosecuted or their punishment. They only record the number of cases that are "placed on file for investigation" and these only cover cases of "torture to extract confessions" (see above). While these figures indicate that some cases are investigated, there is evidence that many are not. Indeed, few of the official reports have ever recorded investigations into cases of "corporal punishment and abuse" of prisoners — even though this is also prohibited by law and there are numerous reports of such abuses. Moreover, since the law clearly limits the scope of official action, they never record cases of torture for reasons other than to "extract confessions".

According to both official and unofficial sources, few cases of torture are investigated and even fewer are prosecuted. Loyalty to colleagues, the importance of local connections, corruption, political pressure and other factors usually determine whether investigations are carried out and, when they are, their outcome. Often, no action is taken to punish perpetrators or else disciplinary sanctions are imposed without a judicial investigation. Chinese procurators, who are responsible for judicial investigations of torture allegations, are often unwilling or powerless to prosecute perpetrators.

There are frequent cover-ups by the authorities. An official newspaper stated a few years ago: "Some basic-level leaders personally witness policemen practising torture to extract confessions but turn a blind eye and let it pass."[41] Official and unofficial sources say that cover-ups are also organized at a high level. In one case reported in the *Legal Daily* on 21 January 1994, three police officers, a village Party Secretary and his brother, who had tortured a young man to death in Hebei province in 1991, remained at large for over two and a half years because of a cover-up by law enforcers "at all levels" in the province. These included the provincial level Public Security authorities. Throughout the two and a half years, the victim's family repeatedly raised the case with the authorities, but no action was taken. It was only investigated after the case was publicized in a legal magazine and caused a public outcry at the lack of official action. This raises doubts as to whether the case would ever have been investigated if it had not been publicized.

Many sources report that few of the cases investigated are prosecuted, as investigations are often dropped and disciplinary sanctions imposed in preference to criminal punishment. These reports would seem to be confirmed by the lack of published official statistics for such prosecutions. In one case in 1993 in Harbin, Heilongjiang province, the provincial Public Security authorities were reported to have obstructed the judicial process so that 17 police officers accused of torturing a man to death remained unpunished for almost two years. According to a Hong Kong magazine,[42] the police officers had been charged with manslaughter, but the case had not been concluded because the police authorities had blocked the judicial process — apparently fearing that any sentencing of the officers might dampen police morale. The victim's family had apparently been put under intense pressure by the authorities to drop the case in exchange for compensation and the provincial governor ordered a news black-out on the case.

In the numerous cases of political prisoners who are reported to have been tortured or ill-treated, the government has usually denied the allegations, claiming that they have been investigated and found to be untrue. However, it has never provided evidence to substantiate such claims. It is unlikely that any criminal investigations, let alone impartial ones, were ever carried out into these cases. Amnesty International has never come across a report of an official being prosecuted for torturing or ill-treating a political prisoner.

Amnesty International believes there are several reasons why so few cases of torture are investigated and prosecuted. They include:

- The limited powers of the procuracies to initiate criminal investigations into torture allegations and the failure of many procurators to take action on all reports of torture.

- The involvement of other authorities in the investigation of torture allegations, including the Public Security (police) agencies themselves, which results in many investigations being dropped without a judicial investigation. The government has confirmed the involvement of the police authorities in the investigation of torture cases, without specifying how such investigations are carried out.[43] This raises doubts about the impartiality of investigations.

- The lack of public scrutiny of the procedures followed during investigation. There are no known procedures stipulated by law on how investigations should be carried out. Nor are there formal procedural safeguards to guarantee the safety of the alleged victims and potential witnesses, such as by transferring the alleged perpetrators. The investigations are not public and their findings are not subject to public scrutiny. As a result, complaints are often withdrawn and investigations dropped.[44]

- Existing provisions in Chinese law prohibit only some acts of torture and ill-treatment, leaving considerable room for interpretation. The loopholes are reflected in practice by a tendency to investigate and prosecute only some of the most serious cases of torture and ill-treatment.

- The fear of reprisals and distrust of the complaints system inhibit many prisoners and their relatives from making complaints. The Convention against Torture requires China to protect complainants against intimidation (Article 14).

The Chinese Government is accountable under Chinese law to curb torture. It also has an international obligation under the Convention against Torture to take effective measures to prevent it. Its failure to do so, and the impunity it offers to many torturers, indicate that torture is in effect tolerated in the exercise of state power.

5

The death penalty

The death penalty is applied arbitrarily in China, frequently as a result of political interference. There are hardly any safeguards to prevent miscarriages of justice.

Thousands of people are sentenced to death every year, often following grossly unfair and summary trials. Many of them are executed shortly after sentencing, usually by a single shot to the back of the head. In 1994 Amnesty International recorded more than 2,780 death sentences and 2,050 executions — three times as many executions as in the rest of the world. During the first half of 1995, the organization recorded some 1,800 death sentences and 1,147 executions in China. These figures, however, which are based on a limited number of published reports, are believed to represent only a fraction of the actual totals. The Chinese authorities do not publish statistics about the death penalty as they treat these as a "state secret".

Amnesty International opposes the death penalty without reservation in all cases, on the grounds that it is the ultimate cruel, inhuman and degrading punishment and violates the right to life as proclaimed in the Universal Declaration of Human Rights and other international human rights instruments.

Amnesty International has long been concerned about the extensive use of the death penalty in China and about many of the ways it is applied. These include the lack of safeguards to prevent miscarriages of justice, the use of summary trial procedures in some death penalty cases, the parading of condemned prisoners before they are executed, the shackling of prisoners while they await execution and the use of organs from executed prisoners for transplants.

Extensive use of the death penalty

The Chinese authorities have long used the death penalty extensively. They have also continued to expand its scope — from an original list of 21 offences under the 1980 Criminal Law, the death penalty now applies to an estimated 68 offences. According to international standards, the death penalty should be used only for the "most serious crimes".[45] The UN Human Rights Committee, a group of experts that monitors implementation of the International Covenant on Civil and Political Rights, has declared that the death penalty "should be a quite exceptional measure". The UN has also called for the worldwide and progressive reduction of crimes carrying the death penalty.

During the first half of 1995, people were executed in China for a wide range of violent and non-violent crimes. These included: murder, attempted murder, manslaughter, armed robbery, robbery, rape, causing injury, assault, habitual theft, theft, burglary,

An increasing number of death sentences have been passed in recent years for non-violent offences and drug-trafficking. This photograph shows prisoners being sentenced to death in Pehong prefecture, Yunnan province, during an anti-drugs campaign. © Xinhua/Frank Spooner

kidnapping, trafficking in women or children, prostitution, pimping, organizing pornography rings, publishing pornography, hooliganism, seriously disrupting public order, causing explosions, destroying or causing damage to public or private property, "counter-revolutionary sabotage", arson, poisoning of livestock, drug-trafficking, killing a tiger, corruption, embezzlement, taking bribes, fraud, speculation and profiteering, forgery, reselling value-added tax receipts, tax evasion, stealing or illegally manufacturing weapons, illegally possessing or selling firearms and ammunition, stealing or dealing in national treasures or cultural relics, selling counterfeit money and blackmail. Others were sentenced to death and may have been executed for gambling, selling fake invoices, causing death through torture, bigamy and misappropriation of public funds.

In recent years, a growing number of people have been sentenced to death for non-violent offences such as theft, as well as for drug-trafficking, and some have been executed for relatively minor offences. In 1994, for instance, two peasants were executed in Henan province for stealing 36 cows and small items of agricultural machinery worth US$ 9,300. According to some sources, a person can be sentenced to death if the "economic loss" involved is 40,000 yuan (about US$ 5,000) or more.

Spates of executions regularly take place before major festivals or events, including the UN Conference on Women in mid-1995, or shortly after the authorities launch crackdowns on crime. A nationwide anti-corruption campaign begun in 1993, for instance, has led to a large number of executions for corruption. This has had no apparent impact on corruption. Local authorities have applied the death penalty to make examples of certain types of offenders who are deemed to pose a problem locally. Thus the same offence can be punished by death in one province and by a term of imprisonment in another.

Death sentences also appear to be used by the authorities to ensure that sensitive policies are carried out. For example, Yu Jian'an, the vice-president of a hospital in Henan province, was executed for reportedly taking bribes in exchange for issuing false sterilization certificates.[46]

Amnesty International is also concerned that minors aged between 16 and 18 can be sentenced to death with a two-year reprieve. Chinese law allows the courts to pronounce death sentences in which execution is suspended for two years "if immediate

Page 88: (top) *an official of the Sichuan Provincial High People's Court confirms the death sentences passed on two arsonists, July 1989, and* (below) *policemen force the men into position for execution.* (Above) *signs are placed on the bodies indicating the crimes and names of the executed prisoners.*
© *Pascal G/Agence Vu*

execution is not essential" (Article 43 of the Criminal Law). In these cases, the prisoners must carry out "reform through labour" during the period of reprieve and their attitude is examined for evidence of "repentance" or "reform". If the prisoner shows appropriate signs of repentance then the sentence may be commuted to life. or fixed-term imprisonment. However, if the prisoner is deemed not to have "reformed", the execution is carried out at the end of the two-year reprieve. Thus, someone who was a minor at the time of the offence can be executed, in flagrant violation of.international standards.[47] Although Chinese official sources claim that most of those sentenced to death with a two-year reprieve have their sentences commuted, they do not publish information on such cases. The fate of many of those who have received "suspended" death sentences remains unknown.

Advocates of the death penalty in China argue that its scope has been expanded to tackle growing crime, including violent and organized crime. However, there is no evidence to show that the extensive use of the death penalty has succeeded in reducing either the crime rate or certain kinds of crime. In fact, there is substantial evidence that all forms of crime have been steadily increasing in China during the past decade, despite increased use of the death penalty. The most recent survey on the relation between the death penalty and homicide rates, conducted for the UN in 1988, concluded that: "This research has failed to provide scientific proof that executions have a greater deterrent effect than life imprisonment".

Summary trials

> "Once a head is chopped off, history shows it can't be restored, nor can it grow again as chives do, after being cut. If you cut off a head by mistake, there is no way to rectify the mistake, even if you want to."[48]
> Mao Zedong, 1956

Judicial errors can occur in any legal system. However, the chances of error are much greater when there is no protection for the rights of the accused, when there is a heavy reliance on confessions, when the outcome of a trial is decided in advance, and when the appeal procedure is a mere formality. In death penalty cases, judicial errors are irreparable.

According to many sources, the procedures in China for trial in death penalty cases are summary and grossly inadequate when a "law and order" campaign is under way. Even at the best of times, Chinese law does not include some of the minimum guarantees for fair trial spelled out in international human rights law (see Chapter 1). International standards make it clear that in death penalty cases there is a special obligation to ensure that the sentence is only imposed "after legal process which gives all possible safeguards to ensure a fair trial".[49]

In addition, some law enforcement and judicial practices, such as the use of torture to extract confessions, may result in wrong convictions in death penalty cases. Examples of innocent people who were executed have occasionally been cited by the Chinese press. For instance, in 1995 Li Xiuwu was declared innocent seven years after he was executed on conviction of murdering a farmer and stealing. Another man, Wei Liguang, was then executed for the same crime after being turned in to the police by associates.

Since 1983 some death penalty cases have been tried under legislation which clearly provides for summary trial procedures. The legislation was adopted on 2 September 1983 at the start of a nationwide "anti-crime campaign" that resulted in thousands of executions within a few weeks. This legislation was also used in the trials of scores of people who were summarily executed in the immediate aftermath of the 4 June 1989 crackdown. It continues to be used today.

The 1983 "Decision of the National People's Congress Standing Committee Regarding the Procedure for Rapid Adjudication of Cases Involving Criminal Elements Who Seriously Endanger Public Security" makes it clear that those to be tried under it are considered guilty before trial. It states that those "criminal elements" on whom death sentences "should be imposed" for offences "seriously endangering public security" should be tried rapidly and promptly "if the major facts of the crime are clear, the evidence is conclusive and they have incurred great popular indignation". The Decision further provides that, in order to speed up trial procedures in such cases, the courts can bring defendants to trial without giving them a copy of the indictment in advance and without giving warning of the trial or serving summonses in advance to all parties involved. This means that defendants can be tried without the assistance of a lawyer and without knowing exactly what accusations they face until they arrive in court. The Decision also reduces the time limit for appeals against a judgment from 10 days to three days.

Prisoners sentenced to death have the right to one appeal against the verdict, but these are rarely successful. Like the trials, they are usually a mere formality. If the defendant does not appeal, Chinese law provides for the case to be reviewed by a court higher than that which passed sentence in the first instance. The CPL, as adopted in 1979, also provided that all death sentences should be submitted to the Supreme People's Court for approval after review by a high court. This procedure, however, has been effectively curtailed in many cases since the early 1980s.

A permanent amendment to the law was introduced in 1983 to speed up the procedure for judicial review and approval in some death penalty cases. It allows the High People's Courts directly to approve some death sentences, instead of the Supreme People's Court. These cases are, as above, those concerning offences which "seriously endanger public security". As the high courts are also the bodies which hear appeals in death penalty cases, this measure means that the procedure for appeal and that for review and approval of the verdict are amalgamated into one, so that in many cases death sentences are approved by the High Court almost

The bodies of several men following execution in Beijing in June 1993.
© *Open Magazine*

immediately after trial and the defendants are executed soon after being sentenced. Moreover, in violation of UN standards, Chinese law does not allow those sentenced to death to seek pardon or commutation of the sentence.

Execution of political activists

Dozens of people were summarily executed in Beijing and elsewhere in the immediate aftermath of the 1989 crackdown.[50] Others were sentenced to death with a two-year reprieve on a mixture of political and criminal charges. For example, five people under suspended death sentences were reported in 1994 to be held at Beijing Prison No. 2 for activities related to the June 1989 protests. They had been convicted of "counter-revolutionary sabotage" or "counter-revolutionary arson" in relation to the destruction of military vehicles and other property on 4 June 1989. Their current fate is unknown.

Several people were sentenced to death in connection with the 1990 "counter-revolutionary rebellion" in Baren township in the west of Xinjiang (see Chapter 3). They included Kurban Mohammed, Sulayman Sopy and Ghopor Awwal, who were reportedly publicly executed in Baren town centre in June 1992.

A number of Muslim nationalists have been executed in

Xinjiang in recent years for alleged involvement in protests, underground political organizations or bombings. On 30 May 1995, for example, the authorities in Xinjiang publicized the execution that day of five Muslim nationalists accused of having planted bombs in Urumqi in 1992, one of which killed three people. Three of those executed were convicted of "causing.explosions" and robbery, and the two others of forming a "counter-revolutionary group" and "counter-revolutionary sabotage". They had allegedly set up a clandestine party, the Islamic Reformers Party, and directed members of the group to rob a bank in order to buy weapons.

Treatment of prisoners sentenced to death

Prisoners sentenced to death are frequently paraded in front of large crowds at "mass sentencing rallies" where their crimes and sentences are publicized. These rallies, and other similar public meetings to announce sentences, usually take place just before the prisoners are taken to the execution ground. In June 1995, for

The deliberate public humiliation of prisoners at "mass sentencing rallies" amounts to cruel and degrading treatment. © Xinhua/Frank Spooner

instance, tens of thousands of people attended mass rallies in several provinces in south China to hear the announcement of death sentences on scores of prisoners convicted of drug-trafficking. The prisoners were executed immediately after the rallies.

During such rallies, the prisoners are usually forced to face the crowd with their head bowed, hands tied behind their back and a placard announcing their name and crimes tied around their neck. Some are gagged to prevent them from shouting out. Prisoners tied in this way are also paraded in open trucks through the streets before they are executed. Amnesty International considers that these practices amount to cruel and degrading treatment.

It is also common practice in China for prisoners sentenced to death to wear handcuffs and leg irons from the time they are sentenced until they are executed. Regulations published in 1982 for prison and labour camp wardens stipulate that "leg irons and handcuffs may be used together on prisoners awaiting execution". Whereas the time limit for wearing shackles is normally 15 days,

A large group of prisoners with placards around their necks at a "mass sentencing rally" in Chengdu city, Sichuan province, in November 1993.
© Teresa Poole

both official and unofficial sources indicate that there is no time limit for their use on prisoners sentenced to death.[51]

Former prisoners have confirmed that it is routine for prisoners sentenced to death to be shackled until they are executed. For example, Chen Gang, a young worker from Xiangtan who had been sentenced to death shortly after his arrest in June 1989, was held at Longxi prison in Hunan province with his hands and feet shackled continuously for about 10 months. The shackles were only taken off when his case was reviewed in April 1990 and his sentence was changed to death with a two-year reprieve. During the same period, at the Guangzhou No.1 Detention Centre, several female prisoners who had had appeals against their death sentences rejected were kept in leg irons for more than a month before they were executed.

The use of leg irons and chains as instruments of restraint is prohibited by international standards. Other restraints such as handcuffs are only allowed in very limited circumstances, such as when prisoners are being moved. The application of leg irons and chains and the prolonged use of other restraints amount to cruel, inhuman or degrading treatment and add to the cruelty of the application of the death penalty.

Use of organs for transplants

The main source of organs for transplants in China is reported to be executed prisoners. There is no system of voluntary donation. It is estimated that up to 90 per cent of transplant kidneys come from executed prisoners. Other organs reportedly taken from executed prisoners include corneas and hearts. According to some reports, foreign nationals can travel to China and buy transplants using organs from executed prisoners.

Details of the organ retrieval process are closely guarded by the Chinese authorities, but information has emerged through security and health personnel involved in the procedure. A medical source interviewed by Amnesty International described the procedure followed when executions were imminent. According to the source, the head of the Intermediate People's Court (which passed the sentences) gave notice of impending executions to the deputy head of the court's executive office, who in turn notified the health department of the relevant local government. The health department then contacted the appropriate hospitals, giving the

number and date of the executions and medical details of the condemned.

Prisoners who are selected to provide organs are given medical examinations. Blood samples are taken, usually without the prisoner being told why the tests are being done. Once the execution has been carried out, the body is usually taken to the designated hospital in an ambulance. Sometimes, the organs are removed from the body immediately in a vehicle parked at the execution ground. Generally, the body is cremated and the ashes returned to the family, who cannot therefore verify if organs have been removed. If the family requests the return of the intact corpse, they are usually given a bill for the prisoner's upkeep during detention, which is often beyond the family's means.

According to Chinese official sources, transplants of organs from executed prisoners only happen if the prisoners or their family give their consent. Regulations in force since 1984 require such consent except when no one claims the body or the prisoner's family "refuses" to claim it. However, despite the regulations and official assurances, many sources concur that transplant organs do not normally come from unclaimed bodies or following consultation with the prisoner's family, and that consent for organ retrieval is rarely sought from the condemned prisoner.

The close liaison between courts, health departments and hospitals over the distribution of transplant organs, the secrecy surrounding the process, the fact that organ transplantation represents a source of income for hospitals, and the reported practice of giving gifts to officials involved in the execution process, all suggest that in some cases the imposition and timing of the death penalty may be influenced by the need for organs for transplantation. The Chinese legal system provides no protection against such abuse.

Inside the walls of Beijing Prison No. 1. © Colorific!

6

China and the world

As China has played an increasingly prominent role in world affairs, the government has been forced to respond to criticism of its human rights record. Yet rather than genuinely attempting to improve protection of human rights, it has appeared to direct much of its effort towards deflecting criticism and avoiding accountability.

Since the widespread condemnation of the gross violations committed during the 1989 crackdown on pro-democracy protests, the government has taken a number of widely publicized human rights initiatives. These have included receiving foreign government delegations to discuss human rights issues, setting up human rights study groups and releasing early a few prisoners of conscience.

To the extent that these initiatives indicate a shift, however small, in official attitudes towards human rights, they are important. Unfortunately, it appears that most of them were merely gestures to appease international opinion. Not one has yet been matched by concrete measures to address widespread and serious human rights violations.

The Chinese Government has stated that it recognizes the universality of UN human rights standards. Yet it also argues that states must be free to implement these standards according to their specific cultural, historical and political circumstances. In practice, such freedom has amounted to a licence for state violations of basic human rights.

The Chinese Government has sought to evade accountability for its human rights record, both externally and internally. Despite its acknowledgement that international dialogue on human rights issues is part of "normal" international relations, it continues to deny the legitimacy of international scrutiny of its human rights record, viewing this as unwarranted interference in China's internal affairs. It has also failed to account fully to UN human rights bodies and monitoring mechanisms, despite its ratification of UN human rights treaties.

The government has frequently accused its critics of exploiting human rights issues for political ends. With some justification, it has also accused some governments of hypocrisy, pointing out that they too are guilty of human rights violations. Such accusations, however, do nothing to mitigate China's own record and suggest that the authorities are seeking to avoid responsibility for their own behaviour.

Internally, the government continues to impede independent human rights monitoring by repressing domestic human rights groups and barring international human rights organizations from visiting China. It vilifies human rights activists at home as "counter-revolutionaries", "anti-Chinese" and "splittists", often harassing them or locking them away for years. The many people who risk their lives daily by demanding respect of their fundamental human rights are not criminals. Nor do they have less right to

A trade zone in Shanghai. © *Tom Stoddart/Katz*

express their views than the government which claims to speak on their behalf.

China's stance on human rights

China joined the international consensus of states which adopted the Vienna Declaration and Programme of Action at the 1993 UN World Conference on Human Rights. The Declaration reaffirmed: "The universal nature of these rights and freedoms [in the UN Charter] is beyond question."

At the same time, the Chinese Government strongly asserts that the principles enshrined in international human rights standards emphasize individual civil and political rights at the expense of collective economic and cultural rights — rights, it argues, that are paramount for the Chinese people. However, international human rights law is not solely concerned with civil and political rights, nor does it deal solely with the rights of the individual. Many of its

China's new skyline: a statue of Chairman Mao Zedong, a pagoda and a satellite dish. © Rhodri Jones/Panos

provisions stress social, cultural and collective rights, and there is recognition of the duties individuals have towards others and the community at large.

The body of international human rights law is not the product of one cultural tradition. It has emerged over the past 50 years from the most international forum the world has ever known, the UN, which at present has 185 member states. Most international human rights instruments, starting with the Universal Declaration of Human Rights (UDHR), have been accepted by the General Assembly where all member states speak and vote.

The Chinese Government's general stance on human rights was clearly spelled out in a "white paper", *Human Rights in China*, published in November 1991. It argued that although the problem of food and clothing had basically been solved and standards of living had risen, China was still a developing country with limited resources and a huge population, where "social turmoil" could threaten the people's most important right — the "right to subsistence". It concluded that preservation of national independence and state sovereignty was fundamental for the survival and development of the Chinese people. This led to the further conclusion that "maintaining national stability" was "a long-term, urgent task" for the government.

Such arguments are a diversion. The Vienna Declaration reaffirmed, "while development facilitates the enjoyment of all human rights, the lack of development may not be invoked to justify the abridgement of internationally recognized human rights." The need to feed the hungry cannot justify committing torture. The white paper gives no evidence, nor is there any from anywhere in the world, that denying people such a fundamental right as freedom of speech promotes or improves their "right to subsistence". No government has the right to pick and choose which fundamental human rights are to be respected — all are universal and indivisible, as China itself recognizes. There is no hierarchy of human rights.

Likewise, the need to "maintain stability" is no justification for repressing the most basic human rights. Indeed, international human rights instruments have been carefully drafted by governments themselves to provide only those minimum human rights guarantees which are compatible with maintaining political stability. Nor does the emphasis on stability justify using double standards in the application of the law and allowing officials to transgress the law with impunity.

The international community does not deny the right of any government to act in the face of real and immediate threats to national security, although even then there are some rights, such as the right not to be tortured, which states can never ignore. But in China "maintaining national stability" has been interpreted by the government to include almost any activity which is seen as a threat to the prevailing power structures. This has meant that people have been killed, tortured and arbitrarily imprisoned for expressing opinions or exchanging information in a perfectly legitimate and peaceful way.

The white paper challenged the fundamental principle that China is accountable before the international community. It confirmed that China was willing to engage in some international cooperation on human rights issues and stated that the government "highly appraised" the UDHR. Yet the paper consistently argued that human rights fall, by and large, within the domestic jurisdiction or "sovereignty" of each country. With such an approach, the Chinese Government has been able to acknowledge in its rhetoric the importance of international human rights standards, while at the same time rejecting in practice any criticism of its human rights record based on these same standards as interference in its internal affairs.

The Chinese Government in effect rejects one of the most remarkable and enduring developments since the founding of the UN: the recognition that there are universal minimum human rights guarantees which all states must abide by and that the international community has a right and duty to hold all states to account if they fail to respect these rights. It is a principle reflected in the development of international human rights law and practice. It is also a principle that was reaffirmed when all UN member states agreed the Vienna document, which proclaimed that "...the promotion and protection of all human rights is a legitimate concern of the international community."

The white paper emphasized that a country's human rights situation should not be judged in isolation from its historical, social, economic and cultural conditions, or "according to a preconceived model" or the conditions of another country or region. Country-specific "conditions", however, can never justify fundamental human rights violations. The Chinese Government apparently recognized this by accepting the Vienna document, which stated: "While the significance of national and regional

particularities and various historical, cultural and religious back-
grounds must be borne in mind, it is the duty of states, regardless
of their political, economic and cultural systems, to promote and
protect all human rights and fundamental freedoms".

Every human being has the right not to be tortured, killed or
arbitrarily detained. These are concrete, not abstract, principles.
They do not vary according to the cultural or political climate. A
black or white prisoner on death row in the USA, a Roman Catholic
or Protestant in Northern Ireland, or a Hutu or Tutsi in Rwanda all
have the right to be safe from state violence. The international
community has agreed that these rights are universal and inalien-
able. They apply to all people in all circumstances.

The majority of the white paper was devoted to detailing the
rights set down in the Chinese Constitution and law. However, the
numerous and daily violations of these rights expose the gap
between law and practice in China — a problem not even mentioned by the paper. It claimed, as do officials, that political prisoners do not exist in China because "ideas alone, in the absence of
action which violates the Criminal Law, do not constitute a crime".
It also claimed that prisoners enjoy many rights and it attacked as
a "groundless fabrication" the "allegation that in China some citizens are sent to labour camps without trial". The evidence in this
report shows that these claims are untrue.

The white paper, along with many other official statements,
indicates that the Chinese Government's human rights policy remains basically unchanged. Human rights are to be respected only
if they are exercised in ways that are deemed not to threaten the
interests of those in power.

The government's refusal to acknowledge that there are serious
human rights problems in China was reinforced by two other "white
papers" issued in 1992. The first, "The Reform of Criminal Offenders in China", rebutted criticisms of prison labour in China and
detailed the rights theoretically enjoyed by prisoners under the law.
The second, "Tibet — Its Ownership and Human Rights Situation",
concentrated on listing the "achievements" made in Tibet in the past
30 years. Neither paper mentioned a single report of human rights
violations or measures to improve human rights protection.

There is ample evidence that many Chinese people do not
subscribe to their government's concept of human rights. As was
shown in Chapter 2, they have tried peacefully to promote alternative views within the narrow confines of the law, only to face

harassment and detention. The victims of China's repressive legislation and officials' abuse of power do not perceive their persecution as a legitimate part of "Chinese culture". They experience it for what it is — a violation of the fundamental rights that are the heritage and entitlement of all humanity.

China, human rights and the UN

The Chinese Government's relationship with the UN in the field of human rights shows that it is willing to accept the legitimacy of international human rights law and international scrutiny of its human rights record — but only to the extent that this does not threaten the existing political order in China or expose the systemic violations of human rights in the country.

China is now a State Party to seven UN human rights treaties[52] and has submitted reports to the UN committees that monitor implementation of some of these treaties. Yet, as this report shows, violations of fundamental rights by state officials remain endemic in China and the government has failed to respond fully to the concerns raised by bodies such as the UN Committee Against Torture (see Chapter 4). Moreover, China has not ratified two of the most important human rights treaties: the International Covenant on Civil and Political Rights (ICCPR) and the International Covenant on Economic, Social and Cultural Rights (ICESCR).

The government has also failed to respond to many inquiries by the mechanisms set up under the UN Commission on Human Rights (UNCHR) that deal with thematic issues such as torture, arbitrary detention and extrajudicial executions. When it has responded to inquiries, such as those from the Special Rapporteur on torture, the answers have generally sought to justify the authorities' actions or simply denied the allegations without corroborative evidence.

In recent years China has stepped up its efforts to participate in the activities of the UN, including in the field of human rights. It has been a member of the UNCHR since 1982 and was Vice-Chair in 1989. It has increasingly sought to shape the UN's human rights work in other arenas. While it has played a positive role in developing aspects of some standards, it has consistently sought to undermine and weaken standards dealing with violations about which it feels vulnerable. Its negative role is clear, for example, in the continuing process of drafting the declaration to protect human

GAO YU
(China)
Prisoner of Conscience

rights defenders. Such actions confirm that the Chinese Government is willing to cooperate on human rights only to the extent that this is not perceived to threaten its political interests or expose the true scale of violations in China.

While supporting human rights scrutiny in some other countries, the Chinese Government maintains its stance of "non-interference" in its own internal affairs. For four consecutive years from 1991, it successfully used a procedural motion to block any resolution critical of its human rights record being debated by the UNCHR. In March 1995, however, China's procedural motion failed. It narrowly escaped censure when a draft resolution on its human rights record was subsequently defeated by just one vote. The use of such procedural ploys to evade scrutiny is deplorable. No state should be immune from examination by the UN's principal human rights body. Any such exemptions would undermine the basic UN principle that all states are bound by the same rules and judged by the same standards.

The Chinese Government has, nevertheless, taken a few small steps towards allowing international scrutiny of its human rights record. In November 1994 the UN Special Rapporteur on religious intolerance, Abdelfattah Amor, visited China, including the TAR, and met several religious leaders. This was the first official visit to the PRC by a UN human rights expert. However, the visit did not represent a major change of policy. The Chinese authorities went to considerable lengths to prevent Abdelfattah Amor from speaking freely to people when he was in China. His meetings were closely controlled by the authorities and some were forbidden. In Tibet, tight security was in force in Lhasa and Tibetans who wanted to give him information were reportedly unable to do so because of police surveillance.

The Fourth World Conference on Women held in Beijing in August and September 1995 also appeared to signal more openness — it was the first major UN conference to be held in China. Yet before and during the conference, Chinese dissidents and relatives of prisoners of conscience were detained, harassed, restricted or placed under 24-hour police surveillance to prevent them from making public statements or contacting foreigners. The government

---

A member of Amnesty International demonstrates at the opening session of the Non-Governmental Organizations Forum on Women, held in June 1995 before the UN Conference on Women, Beijing. © Hulton/Reuters

also restricted non-governmental organizations (NGOs) to a specially designated area far from Beijing. It prevented members of some independent Chinese NGOs from attending and closely controlled the activities of those allowed to attend.

No government should be allowed to choose the extent to which it will abide by international human rights law. No government should be allowed to manipulate human rights issues to further its political aims. To work within the UN means accepting the universality of the fundamental human rights spelled out in the UDHR as well as the application in all countries of the laws, bodies and mechanisms which aim to protect those rights.

This is particularly relevant for China, which is one of the five permanent members of the UN Security Council and thereby has considerable influence and responsibility to uphold the UN Charter. If China is to be an active and full member of the international community, it must accept the greater accountability and openness that comes with that membership.

While many governments and non-governmental organizations have condemned the continuing gross violations of human rights in China, the idea that the international community is doing all it can to exert pressure on the Chinese Government about human rights does not stand up to close examination. On many occasions, governments have buckled under political pressure not to criticize China. The UNCHR failed to pass a single resolution condemning the massacre of civilians during the 1989 crackdown or the many subsequent violations of human rights across the country.

For the international community, the issue of action in relation to the continuing gross human rights violations in China is a question of political will and vision. The Chinese Government has shown it is not insensitive to world opinion. It is time for the international community to exert sustained pressure on the Chinese authorities to abide by human rights norms. Governments should act to ensure that China is open to scrutiny by, and dialogue with, the thematic experts of the UNCHR, including the Special Rapporteur on torture, the Working Group on arbitrary detention and the Special Rapporteur on extrajudicial, summary or arbitrary executions. China should be encouraged to ratify, without limiting reservations, the ICCPR and its two optional protocols, and the ICESCR.

Relations with the ICRC and international human rights organizations

The Chinese Government has also sought to avoid scrutiny for its human rights performance by preventing independent human rights monitors from working in the country. The International Committee of the Red Cross (ICRC), for example, has been negotiating with the Chinese authorities for many years to be allowed to visit Chinese prisons. According to its procedures, the ICRC requires unaccompanied and unimpeded meetings with any prisoners in any prison to ensure that they can speak freely. It also sets other conditions to ensure the safety of the prisoners it meets. Although the ICRC only discusses its findings confidentially with the government concerned, the Chinese Government has so far refused to accept its requirements for prison visits.

Hopes that such visits might take place were raised in 1993 — at the time China presented a bid to host the 2000 Olympic Games — when the Chinese Foreign Minister, Qian Qichen, announced that China had in principle agreed to ICRC inspections. In early 1995, however, a Chinese Ministry of Justice official said that China would not accept the ICRC's standard requirements for prison visits and stated that such pre-conditions were "hardly feasible for China."[53]

International human rights organizations have also tried unsuccessfully to obtain official access to China. In 1993 the *Fédération internationale des droits de l'homme* (International Federation of Human Rights) was promised such a visit by a Chinese official, but the promise has remained unfulfilled.

Amnesty International has sought official access to China to discuss its concerns many times over the years, but has received no response. The government has stated on several occasions that it considers Amnesty International to be "biased" against China. On 2 June 1995, following the publication of an Amnesty International report on China, Foreign Ministry spokesman Chen Jian told a press conference in Beijing: "Amnesty International has always harboured a deep prejudice against China and has been attacking China for no apparent reason." A similar statement was made by the spokesman in September 1995, while an Amnesty International delegation was present in Beijing to attend the UN Fourth World Conference on Women. The delegation had sought meetings with Chinese government officials before it arrived and made further attempts to seek such meetings while in Beijing, but these failed. In September 1995 the authorities denied or cancelled the visas of Amnesty International representatives who were due to attend an international anti-corruption conference in Beijing, even though they had been officially invited by a Chinese institution hosting the conference.

Amnesty International is an independent, non-political, international human rights organization which reports impartially on human rights violations within its mandate in all countries in the world, whatever their political system. It regularly sends delegations to countries to investigate human rights issues or to hold talks with government officials, groups or institutions, in order to secure a wide range of views and information about human rights issues in the countries concerned. As yet, the authorities in China are not allowing such visits or dialogue to take place.

Any country that prevents independent domestic as well as international scrutiny of its human rights record gives the impression that it has much to hide. In the case of China, the secrecy has not prevented reports of gross human rights violations from reaching the outside world, although it does suggest that the scale of human rights violations may be far worse than can be documented. The secrecy also suggests that the Chinese authorities still believe they can do what they like to people and are not accountable for their actions, either internally or externally.

7

Conclusions and recommendations

Despite increased economic freedom in China today, human rights violations continue on a massive scale. They range from harassment or detention of those perceived as a threat to the established order, to gross violations of the physical integrity of the person and the right to life. These violations are caused by official policies, repressive legislation, the system of administrative detention and arbitrary exercise of power by officials. They are encouraged by long-established practices in law enforcement and the judicial process which curtail the individual rights guaranteed by the Chinese Constitution and law.

Recommendations to the government

1. Establish a national commission of inquiry
Amnesty International believes that a fundamental review of legislation and of law enforcement and judicial practices is needed to curb human rights violations in China. The establishment of a national commission of inquiry into human rights would, in Amnesty International's view, provide an opportunity for a thorough review of the circumstances in which human rights abuses occur and the legal and other remedies needed to eradicate them. Article 71 of the Constitution empowers the National People's Congress and its standing committee to appoint committees of inquiry into specific questions and adopt relevant resolutions in the light of their reports.

Pending such a review, other effective measures should be taken without delay to stop the growing number of serious human rights violations. Amnesty International urges the Chinese authorities to consider the following measures which it believes would contribute to the remedy of past and present human rights violations and prevent them recurring.

2. End impunity and compensate victims of human rights violations

To end impunity, Amnesty International urges the authorities to:

- thoroughly, promptly and impartially investigate the circumstances of death of all victims of extrajudicial executions, including those related to the 4 June 1989 crackdown on pro-democracy protests and to pro-independence demonstrations in Tibet in 1988 and 1989;

- ensure that all reports or complaints of torture, other ill-treatment and deaths in custody are thoroughly, promptly and impartially investigated by competent authorities and experts who are not involved in the process of arrest, detention or interrogation of detainees; make the findings of these investigations public and ensure that alleged torturers are brought to justice whenever there are reasonable grounds to believe that an act of torture has been committed;

- ensure that all suspected perpetrators of human rights violations are brought to justice and that, pending the outcome of the proceedings, they are suspended from any position of authority and from all duties in which they have contact with detainees or others at risk of human rights violations;

- ensure that fair compensation is provided to victims of human rights violations or, if the victims have been killed, to their relatives.

3. Stop and prevent torture

To reduce the incidence of torture, Amnesty International urges the authorities to:

- grant detainees prompt and regular access to relatives, and to lawyers and doctors of their choice;

- stop the use of electric batons during interrogation and in custody;

- ban leg-shackles and chains, and strictly limit the use of other instruments of restraint and solitary confinement;

- ensure that officials of all detention and penal institutions prevent ill-treatment of prisoners by "cell bosses" and "prison trustees", and that those delegating supervisory authority to "trusted" prisoners are accountable when other prisoners are tortured or ill-treated as a result. End the use of prisoners to discipline or punish other prisoners.

To prevent torture in the long term, Amnesty International urges the authorities to review legislation so as to:

- prohibit all acts which constitute torture and cruel, inhuman or degrading treatment or punishment, in conformity with the UN Convention against Torture and Other Cruel, Inhuman or Degrading Treatment or Punishment;

- ensure that regulations on the discipline and punishment of prisoners conform with international standards for the treatment of prisoners, particularly with regard to the use of instruments of restraint and solitary confinement;

- introduce a clear separation of authority between the bodies responsible for detention and those in charge of interrogation, as well as procedures to ensure the safety of prisoners during interrogation and custody;

- introduce fundamental legal safeguards for the rights of all detainees and prisoners, including placing limits on incommunicado detention, in line with international standards, and granting detainees prompt and regular access to relatives, and to lawyers and doctors of their choice;

- introduce procedures to ensure that all detainees are brought before a judicial authority promptly after being taken into custody and that this authority can effectively continue to supervise the legality and conditions of detention;

- prohibit the use as evidence in court of statements extracted under torture, in line with Article 15 of the Convention against Torture and Other Cruel, Inhuman or Degrading Treatment or Punishment;

- introduce effective procedures to enable prisoners or their families or lawyer to make complaints about prisoners' treatment and have them considered without fear of reprisals, and to protect them and witnesses from any coercion or intimidation.

4. End arbitrary detention and imprisonment

To end arbitrary detention and imprisonment, Amnesty International urges the authorities to:

- release immediately and unconditionally all prisoners of conscience — those held for the non-violent exercise of their fundamental human rights;

- ensure that all those detained without charge in connection with their alleged political or religious activities are charged with a recognizably criminal offence in accordance with international standards and brought to trial fairly and in a reasonable time, or released;

- immediately after detention notify the relatives of all detainees of the grounds for detention and their whereabouts, and keep relatives regularly informed of any transfer or change in the legal status of the detainees;

- ensure the prompt and impartial review of the trials of all those sentenced after unfair political trials, or release them.

To prevent arbitrary detention and imprisonment in the long term, Amnesty International urges the authorities to:

- amend or repeal all provisions in criminal legislation, including state security and state secrets legislation, which allow for the detention or imprisonment of people who peacefully exercise fundamental human rights;

- ensure that all executive decrees and regulations providing for administrative detention no longer contravene fundamental national legislation and international law;

- review criminal procedure legislation to ensure it provides unambiguous and effective safeguards against arbitrary detention, in line with international human rights standards, in particular by ensuring that:

  — all those detained or arrested are informed immediately of the grounds for their detention and promptly informed of any charges against them, and that their relatives are promptly informed of the place of and grounds for their detention, and of any transfer and change in their legal status;

— anyone deprived of their liberty is held in an officially recognized place of detention and can challenge their detention before an independent judicial authority without delay;

— strict time limits are placed on the duration of preliminary detention before formal arrest and of pre-trial investigation, and that clear procedures are introduced to ensure that these limits are enforced.

5. Ensure fair trials

To ensure fair trials, in accordance with international standards, for political prisoners and those charged with capital offences, Amnesty International urges the authorities to review criminal procedure legislation so as to:

- guarantee detainees regular access to lawyers of their choice well before trial and guarantee adequate time and facilities to prepare a defence and appeals against verdict and sentence;

- ensure that trials are held without undue delay and are open to the public, and guarantee the defence's right to present testimony and cross-examine witnesses for the prosecution;

- introduce the principle of presumption of innocence and ensure that defendants are not compelled to testify against themselves or to confess guilt;

- ensure that Article 123 of the Criminal Procedure Law is not used by judges to prejudice the rights of the defence when the prosecution's evidence is unclear or insufficient for conviction;

- review the role of the courts' adjudication committees to ensure that they do not influence the outcome of trials.

6. Stop the use of the death penalty

To review the extensive use of the death penalty and stop the widespread human rights violations which result from it, Amnesty International urges the authorities to:

- stop all executions;

- abolish the death penalty and commute all outstanding death sentences, including those passed with a two-year reprieve.

Pending abolition, the following measures should be introduced to reduce the practice or mitigate it:

— stop imposing the death penalty on people who were minors at the time of the offence;

— abolish 1983 legislation which introduced summary procedures for the trial, appeal and review of cases liable to the death penalty for offences which "seriously endanger public security";

— end the use of shackles and other restraints on prisoners sentenced to death, and amend regulations which provide for their use;

— end the practice of parading in public prisoners under sentence of death at mass rallies or other events;

— stop the use of organs from executed prisoners for transplants.

7. Stop abuses resulting from the birth control policy
Amnesty International takes no position on the official birth control policy. However, in view of reports of serious human rights violations resulting from the manner of its enforcement, Amnesty International urges the authorities to:

- explicitly prohibit in published regulations the use of coercive methods during birth control enforcement that result in human rights violations;

- take effective measures to ensure that officials who order, perpetrate or acquiesce in such violations are brought to justice.

8. Protect human rights defenders
Amnesty International urges the government to:

- end police and other official harassment or intimidation of human rights defenders, and release human rights defenders who are detained or imprisoned;

- allow all human rights defenders, including members of independent human rights groups, to monitor human rights openly and to have contact with international organizations, without hindrance and with the full protection of the law.

9. Ratify international human rights instruments

Amnesty International urges the government to:

- sign and ratify the International Covenant on Civil and Political Rights (ICCPR), its (first) Optional Protocol which permits the Human Rights Committee to receive individual complaints, its Second Optional Protocol which requires States Parties to take all necessary steps to abolish the death penalty, and the International Covenant on Economic, Social and Cultural Rights (ICESCR).

10. Cooperate with UN human rights mechanisms

To ensure the full and effective implementation of international human rights instruments ratified by China and to demonstrate its commitment to promoting international standards, Amnesty International urges the government to:

- recognize the competence of the UN Committee Against Torture to receive individual complaints (Article 22), to hear inter-state complaints (Article 21) and to investigate reliable information about the systematic practice of torture (Article 20);

- provide full and prompt replies to requests for information by the thematic human rights mechanisms set up under the UN Commission on Human Rights;

- invite the UN Special Rapporteur on torture, the UN Special Rapporteur on extrajudicial, summary or arbitrary executions and the UN Working Group on arbitrary detention to visit China and grant them unrestricted access.

Recommendations to UN member states

In view of the grave concern about human rights in China which has been expressed in a variety of international forums, Amnesty International calls on UN member states to:

1. Urge the Government of the PRC to invite the UN Special Rapporteur on torture, the UN Special Rapporteur on extrajudicial, summary or arbitrary executions, and the UN Working Group on arbitrary detention to visit China.

2. Ensure the regular and effective monitoring of the human rights situation in China by UN human rights bodies.

3. Urge the Chinese Government to allow independent domestic organizations and relevant international organizations to monitor the human rights situation in China.

4. Encourage the Chinese Government to sign and ratify the ICCPR, its Optional Protocols and the ICESCR, and to recognize the competence of the UN Committee Against Torture to receive individual complaints and to hear inter-state complaints.

5. Ensure that asylum-seekers are not forcibly returned to China if they risk serious human rights violations there, and ensure that the claims of all asylum-seekers, including those in detention, are fully and impartially assessed.

ENDNOTES

[1] "Legal system too weak to stop catastrophe", Comment by Zhang Weiguo published in the *South China Morning Post* (SCMP), 4 June 1993. Zhang Weiguo is a former Beijing Bureau chief of the now defunct Shanghai newspaper *World Economic Herald*. He was detained after the 1989 crackdown, released in early 1991, and was permitted to leave China in 1993.

[2] See, in particular Amnesty International's report, *China: Punishment Without Crime — Administrative Detention* (AI Index: ASA 17/27/91), published in 1991.

[3] Principle II of the UN Body of Principles for the Protection of All Persons under Any Form of Detention or Imprisonment.

[4] Speech before the Meeting on Legalisation of Public Security Work, cited in "Criminal Justice with Chinese Characteristics", Lawyers Committee for Human Rights, New York, May 1993, p.70.

[5] See, for example, *Zhongwai Faxue*, Beijing University Law Journal, 1992, No. 4, pages 55-63.

[6] This is distinct from "reform through labour", which applies to prisoners convicted and sentenced to terms of imprisonment under the Criminal Law.

[7] See the case of Fu Shenqi, in Amnesty International's report, *China: Dissidents detained Since 1992* (AI Index: ASA 17/05/94), published in 1994.

[8] For further details, see Human Rights Watch/Human Rights in China, "Leaking State Secrets": the case of Gao Yu, Vol. 7, No. 8, 1995; and Amnesty International's report, *China: Journalist Gao Yu jailed for six years after a secret trial* (AI Index: ASA 17/36/94), November 1994.

[9] See *China: The Massacre of June 1989 and its Aftermath* (AI Index: ASA 17/09/90), April 1990, pp. 50-53.

[10] See "Criminal Justice with Chinese Characteristics", op. cit., p. 56.

[11] Work Report of the Supreme People's Procuratorate to the National People's Congress (NPC), 13 March 1995, in Summary of World Broadcasts (SWB) FE/2269 S2/1, 4 April 1995.

[12] "Work Report of the Supreme People's Court presented by Ren Jianxin", SWB FE/2264 SI/1, 29 March 1995.

[13] The SCMP, 10 May 1994; for further details about those arrested in Shanghai, see *Appeal for human rights activists detained in Shanghai* (AI Index: ASA 17/21/94), 25 May 1994, and *China: Dissidents detained without charge or trial since 1994* (AI Index: ASA 17/02/95), February 1995.

[14] For further details, see *China: Dissidents detained since 1992*, op. cit.

[15] See *Appeal on behalf of Hu Hai* (AI Index: ASA 17/38/92), June 1992. Hu Hai was released in 1993, following repeated appeals by his son and others.

[16] See "Reform and Resistance in China", by Lau Kin Chi, in *Asian Biannual Bulletin of ARENA*, Vol.10, No.1, 1994, p.15.

[17] Many Tibetans also live in parts of China outside the Tibet Autonomous Region.

CHINA

[18] See *Repression in Tibet 1987-1992* (AI Index: ASA 17/19/92); *Torture in China* (AI Index: ASA 17/55/92), December 1992; and *Persistent Human Rights Violations in Tibet* (AI Index: ASA 17/18/95), May 1995.

[19] The SCMP, 3 July 1995.

[20] "First political prisoners still a cause of fear", *Eastern Express*, Hong Kong, 28 to 29 May 1994.

[21] See *Women in China: Imprisoned and abused for dissent* (AI Index: ASA 17/29/95), June 1995.

[22] *The Southern Daily (Nanfang Ribao)*, a newspaper in south China, 6 August 1993.

[23] See the Work Report of the Supreme People's Procuratorate to the NPC, op. cit.

[24] *Liaoning Daily*, 21 May 1995, and Legal Daily, 15 June 1995.

[25] Amnesty International has not come across any other press reports citing official statistics for deaths owing to torture since March 1995. A particularly large number of reports of torture appeared in the Chinese press in 1993, apparently following government instructions the previous year to crack down hard on torture. At the time, China was preparing to submit a report to the UN Committee Against Torture. The March 1993 Supreme People's Procuratorate (SPP) report to the NPC referred to the crackdown on torture and cited 1,687 cases of police and justice officials who had been investigated for using torture to extract confessions between 1988 and 1992.

[26] See *Agence France Presse*, Beijing, 15 October 1993.

[27] *Yangcheng Wanbao (Yangcheng Evening News)*, 8 June 1993.

[28] *Sichuan Daily*, 30 May 1995.

[29] *Shanxi Ribao*, 28 December 1994, and Nongmin Ribao, 22 February 1995.

[30] See *Torture in China*, op. cit.; *China: Update on Torture* (AI Index: ASA 17/12/93), March 1993; and Human Rights Watch/Asia and Human Rights in China, Vol.6, No.5, 1995.

[31] See *People's Republic of China: Persistent human rights violations in Tibet* (AI Index: ASA 17/18/95), May 1995; *People's Republic of China: 123 political arrests in Tibet in three months* (AI Index: ASA 17/27/95), May 1995; and PRC: *Crackdown on Tibetan dissent continues* (AI Index: ASA 17/74/95), September 1995.

[32] *China News and Church Report*, 24 March 1995; see also *News Network International — News Service*, 24 March 1995.

[33] See *Torture in China*, op. cit., pp. 10-14.

[34] See *China: Human rights violations five years after Tiananmen* (AI Index: ASA 17/20/94), June 1994, pp. 21-29.

[35] See *Torture in China*, op. cit., p. 30.

[36] See *Torture in China*, op. cit., and *China: Update on Torture* (AI Index: ASA 17/12/93), March 1993.

[37] Reported in the Brazilian weekly magazine Istoe, 20 July 1994.

[38] See Amnesty International Urgent Action, UA 435/94 (AI Index: ASA 17/38/94), 7 December 1994.

[39] See *Medical concern: Deaths of female ex-prisoners — People's Republic of China (Tibet)*, (AI Index: ASA 17/38/95), June 1995.

[40] The Convention against Torture itself requires China to keep under "systematic review" its interrogation rules and practices as well as the way it treats anyone detained or imprisoned (Article 11).

[41] *People's Public Security News*, 29 September 1991.

[42] *Frontline Magazine*, May 1993, cited in the SCMP of 6 May 1993.

[43] See China's additional report to the UN Committee Against Torture, UN document CAT/C/7/Add.14, para. 67 and 103.

[44] International standards require prompt and impartial investigation into any death in custody and into allegations of torture, and detail how investigations should be carried out.

[45] UN "Safeguards guaranteeing protection of the rights of those facing the death penalty" (ECOSOC death penalty safeguards), approved by Economic and Social Council, 25 May 1984, Resolution 1984/50. See also Article 6 (2) of the International Covenant on Civil and Political Rights (ICCPR).

[46] See *China: Death penalty figures recorded for 1994* (AI Index: ASA 17/17/95), March 1995.

[47] See Article 6 (5) of the ICCPR and Article 3 of the ECOSOC death penalty safeguards.

[48] Mao Zedong, "On the Ten Major Relationships", 1956, in *Selected Works of Mao Zedong*, Vol. 5, Beijing, 1977, pp. 299-300.

[49] Article 5 of the ECOSOC death penalty safeguards.

[50] See *The Massacre of June 1989* and its Aftermath, op. cit., pp. 54-57.

[51] An article in the China *Legal News* of 15 February 1985 confirmed that this was the practice. It stated: "Both implements may be applied simultaneously to criminals sentenced to death and awaiting execution... Apart from the case of condemned criminals awaiting execution, the period of application of handcuffs or ankle-fetters must not exceed a maximum of 15 days."

[52] These are: the Convention against Torture and Other Cruel, Inhuman or Degrading Treatment or Punishment, ratified in 1988; the Convention on the Rights of the Child, ratified in 1992; the Convention on the Elimination of All Forms of Discrimination against Women, ratified in 1980; the International Convention on the Elimination of All Forms of Racial Discrimination, acceded to in 1981; the Convention relating to the Status of Refugees and the Protocol to the Convention relating to the Status of Refugees, both acceded to in 1982; the Convention on the Prevention and Punishment of the Crime of Genocide, ratified in 1983; and the International Convention on the Suppression and Punishment of the Crime of Apartheid, acceded to in 1983.

[53] Cited in the SCMP, 28 January 1995.